Al-Komur Market

Tales and social studies about the River Nile
and Sahara Desert in the Sudanese culture.

By
Professor/ Omar Mahmoud Saeed

I

This book is a publication of:
Create space
49 LaCross Rood
North Charleston, SC 29406
© 2015 by Omar M. Saeed
ISB # 978-0-692-39372-7

The paper used in this publication meets the minimum requirements of the American national Standard for Information Science.

Manufactured in the United State of America.

Library of Congress Cataloging-in-publication Data
Omar, M. Saeed
Includes bibliographical references and index.
The library of Congress Copyright Office
101 Independence Ave., S.E
Washington, D.C. 20559-6000
Certificate of Registration
Registration number:
ISBN-TXU 1-333-146
Dec.28/2006
Receipt No185960
Title: Sohk Al-Komur
Auther E-Mail omarkomur @yahoo.com

Acknowledge
My Friend: Ahmad Gubrial
The translator

The cover design by the auther

The Nile River of Africa and the Sahara
Desert of the Arabs and their impact on the
Sudanese identity

Desert as Father Nile River as Mother

Dedication
To my father and mother with compliments

In Souk (market) Al-Kumur's book there are social tales and natural studies stemming from the human being, nature, and art. It contains cultural models representing various villages located between the cataracts of the Great Nile and other hamlets that drink from the Nile and the Desert or from either of them.

Between the Sahara Desert and the Great River Nile in northern Sudan, Al-Kumur village was built on a broad basin and vast extension of sand where armies of water, sand, and wind wrestle to win them.

The Desert came down with beliefs on sands and trot of camels (tales of beauty); whereas water menstruated from the womb of Africa variety of oysters and fruits.

Between the movement of nature and Al-Kumur's human being, customs developed and sand beliefs and mountain alluvium came down to Souk Al-Kumur. And from the African and Arab groups came some sort of eloquence, rhetoric, and language of wisdom, poetry, and art.

index

Why Write About Souk Al-Kumur?

Human being ever desired to subdue nature for his good; that act caused the struggle between them. There is a struggle in Al-Kumur region between nature itself –the Nile and the Desert. The Nile floods every year to irrigate and protect its basin from floods of valleys coming down with water and sand. As a result, Al-Kumur - down the village and Souk - witnesses a fierce battle between alluvium and sand.

The village of Al-Kumur, its Souk (market), and surrounding villages are abounding in tales and traditions, which originated from the land of Africa or came from the Arabian Peninsula.

Between the village and the Souk human being grows with his traditions related to nature of the Nile or Desert. These traditions struggle and merge to come down on the plain of Souk Al-Kumur in the shape of another commodity. Traditions as all other commodities also divide. Poetry, jokes, and animals and birds of land and sea also follow suit.

Preface (1)

Tributaries pour into the Blue Nile and others flow in the White Nile. The two Niles (Blue and White) meet at the confluence near Khartoum where they mix and collaborate in making their way in the Nubian Desert, northern Sudan, after forming the Great River Nile.

The Nile heads north. At Jabals (mountains) Rawyan and Atshan, it collides with the Desert, mixes with it, and irrigates its soil. It overpasses the rocks of the 1st Cataract to change its course eastwards.

The Nubian Desert is a branch of the Sahara Desert and a sand valley that runs between mountains and River Nile.

Inhabitants of the Sahara lead their daily life climbing mountains or going down to the Nile's course. Thus the life is divided between the Nile, the Sahara desert, and mountain.

Inhabitants of Al-Kumur village and its surroundings represent the nature of the Nile or the Desert as they are distinguished by customs, which their Nile or Desert lines intersect. This applies to villages located between the 1st and the 6th Cataracts – from Al-Hugnah to Aswan.

Preface (2)

Al-Kumur is one of scattered villages on the western bank of the River Nile, between the 1st and 2nd cataracts, if we number the cataracts according to the flow of River Nile.

Writing about Souk Al-Kumur means writing pages of the social village library.

Nile villages on the verge of the Desert look alike in elements of nature; and man's life is formed of various migrations through history.

Nature migrated, before man, by the migration of sands from the Arabian Desert (Sahara Desert) to the land of Africa to halt its advancement beside the River Nile.

Water and sand are still jostling. So expressions of life refer to the nature of the Nile, Desert, or a blend of the two. Cultures of nature collide and reconcile on the division of water and sand in northern Sudan; on the land of the Nubian kingdoms.

Life divides on the land of the Nile and cataracts, between the Arab and African values, which formed a joint heritage that constituted an integral part in the Sudanese culture and was formed of nature's glow in the mind of man. It is worthy of being published and highlighted because of the nature of the Nile and Desert.

The struggle grew fierce in Al-Kumur region between elements of sand and alluvium. Al-Kurwat came out with the Nile alluvium and floods of valleys came down with sand. Between them Al-Kumur - rich in nature - was founded, which consequently enriched the social, literary, and artistic life.

Dear reader, the village and the human being are the constant and variable in the Sudanese culture; and they are the two elements that lead meanings of life to origins and sources.

I hope you take Souk Al-Kumur's book and its tales as a story, academic study, or select from the chapters what you desire. There is information about the effect of the Nile and Desert's nature on man's life.

The nature of the Nile and Desert is an indication to the life of the Nile's human being in ancient Sudan, Arab Sudan after the ancient Nubian kingdoms, modern Sudan with its present borders, style of life on the River Nile - in the middle and northern Sudan - and the contents of the Sudanese culture in general that mingled between the Nile and the Desert.

The book contains fourteen chapters. The introduction tackled the general presentation. But details are contained inside.

Introduction

Al-Kumur is a village in northern Sudan, in Matamah Province, Shandi District, and one of a group of villages sited between the 1st and 2nd cataracts west of the Nile. It is near the 1st cataract, if we number the cataracts according to the flow of the Nile from south to north.

Houses of Al-Kumur Village are built of mud on the edge of the desert, separated from the muddy lands by a narrow sand strip where farms and escarpments appear on the bank of the great River Nile that springs from the heart of Africa. Behind the houses extends the Desert, which if we follow, will lead us deep in the Arabian Peninsula, home of our ancestors.

Al-Kumur is built on heights at the end of the inclination and estuary of Abu Hawiyah valley into the Nile. The site of Al-Kumur, which lies on crossroads, was the reason behind its foundation. The British colonizers chose this site to build a big Souk (market). Another reason is its vast agricultural lands. Floods also attracted inhabitants to the islands, especially the flood of 1946 (Al-Tasab) which drove part of Nasri island inhabitants, who were fond of their island - surrounded by the Nile - and the island's ways of living.

Why speak about Al-Kumur village? Because it is in the realm of violent natural struggle between the Nile and Desert, which grows fiercer every year between August and September.

Three valleys pour down from top of the mountains. These valleys are: Abu Hawiyah; Eed (group of wells and basins where livestock drink water) Um Zoar, to the right of Abu-Hawiyah; and to the left is Wedi Al-Qubah (Wedi is diminution of valley, and Al-Qubah is a dome built on the tomb of a jurist, a member of Al-Biraiyab tribe, which the region is called after it).

At the estuary of Abu Hawiyah, sand slows down and ends up into the Nile. Some of it, metaphorically, gets older and hence whiter; some mixes with mud and gets blacker;

some is swallowed by the River Nile, between Al-Karo and Um Bagarah in Khor (gorge) Mohyiddeen (Al-Saqai), which represents the Desert natural gap in the body of the Nile.

By following the fabric of villages and songs of nature and human beings on west and south of the bank of the Nile, we anchor in the heart of Africa, vivid with water. If we head eastwards, we can kneel down our camels in the Desert of the Arabian Peninsula.

The Nile breathes every year. During the inhalation its chest goes up and fends off the sand of the valleys. Between the Nile breathing and sand surge, Al-Kumur inhabitants lead their life. One time, the sand covers the neck of the muddy lands; and sometimes, sand dunes swallow the deep water of the banks.

This natural struggle, between the Nile basin and sand valleys, goes on annually at the gates of Al-Kumur Village and at the sight of its inhabitants. It is the subject of my

discourse and writings.   Al-Komur Market
(By: Omar Saeed.)

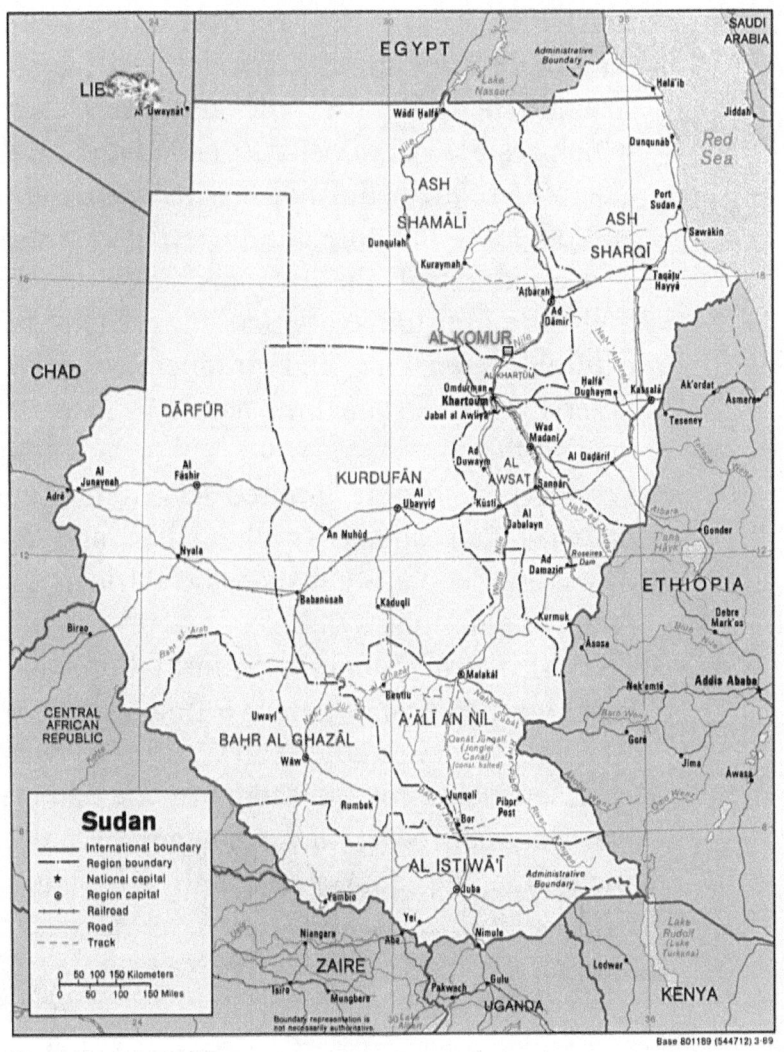

XXIII

1. Al-Kumur and the Struggle of Nature

Al-Kumur region is characterized by a struggle between the Nile and the Desert, which resulted in divisions of sand and mud. Customs related to sand, desert, and Arabs; and others to the Nile and the African basin. The mixture of the two soils led to the Sudanese customs, which deepened the natural dimensions and produced a social diversity that enriched the nature of land and man's life.

Wonderful!! Nature granted Al-Kumur four galaxies that appear to the north and are distributed equally between the African and Arabic names and symbols.

The Afro-Arab topography formations start from west to east, where we find valleys of Al-Karo (a dry muddy soil), Abu Hawiyah (a desert name for the saddle of the camel), Um Bagarah (cow), and Abu Jamal (camel) anchorage. Of course Bagarah (cow) is a Nile animal and the camel is a desert animal.)

2. Geographical Nature of Al-Kumur

The Nile and the Desert struggle acquired Al-Kumur a geographical diversity that widened the spread of banks and islands and formed mountains, valleys, and creeks. Nature mixed Arabic and African lives, from which the combination of names and tribes ramified.

The land heaved and its nature changed with the struggle. The life of the human being had also been affected. Population increased and people intermixed by marriage and migrations due to external wars in the era of the Turkish and British colonization; and internal wars during the rule of Al-Mahadiyah. Events took place, but the region kept coherent and the centripetal force drove people to inside.

The impact of external and internal wars was clear in the intermixing of the region's population in the Turkish era, after Al-Mak Nimer's men killed Ismael bin Mohammed Ali Pasha in Shindi and the consequent

Dafterdar retaliatory campaign on inhabitants of Al-Matamah region.

Afterwards, the region was affected by the campaign Al-Khalifah (Caliph) Abdullah Al-Ta'yshi led by Mohamoud Wad Ahmed on Al-Matamath, which followed by the access of the British colonization.

These wars rocked the region and influenced the composition of population by migration of people between Al-Matamah Village and the 1st cataract passing through Al-Kumur, as it was sited in the middle. Inhabitants of the Nile, Desert, and Mountain shared tragedies of wars; and the nature of land brought them together.

3. The Nile's March and Desert's Advancement

This chapter tackles the meeting of the White Nile with the Blue Nile at the confluence, formation of the River Nile, and the beginning of access to the Desert. Hence the terms of Nile and Desert start at Jabels (mountains) Al-Rawyan and Al-Atshan.

Waters collide and roar at the 1st cataract. The Nile course changes from northward to eastward. At Al-Kumur the struggle of the two giants get fiercer and fiercer.

Ancestors spoke about two courses of the Nile where Al-Kumur is located in between in an area divided equally between the Nile and Desert under the feet of the two wrestlers. The wrestling resulted in land of Afro-Arab topography parallel to the Nile and inhabited by the Arabs of the banks.

The land swayed to form tributaries, valleys, and mountains. The Desert came nearer and the Nile, as it was swaying and approaching from the west carrying the goods of the south to the east on wanton waves colored with the twilight, sagged under Al-Kumur as it rolled. Thus wrestling renews between sand waves and gleeful Nile.

4. Al-Kumur and the Flood of Memories
Here I will speak about the effect of nature in the upbringing of children, the adherence to the birthplace, and how the childhood

playing enriches the hearts of the young. The compositions of imagination and creation are only a flood of proofs of places and nature's volcanoes in the minds of youths.

The making of poetry, creation, and prose of tales in the society are plants from the heart of nature irrigated by families from the present and history of the distant past.

I dealt with two well-known games: Al-Seeja and Al-Tab and spoke about statistics, possibilities, and affiliation to those two games as a model. As information migrate in cases of history and times, selves are also filled with melancholies as a result of leaving homelands.

Al-Kumur generations suffered from both immigrations and nature's struggle till it shouted loud " I am from the Nile and the Desert." It is established on the Desert beside the Nile. The Desert is divided into valleys; and the human being sided with the bank or creeks. A dialogue can be held with the place, between the village and human being.

5. Social Life in Al-Kumur

I spoke in this chapter about Al-Kumur village and neighboring villages that formed one society, about the social characters influencing the daily course of life and Souk Al-Kumur as a social and informational identity.

I also tackled the impact of expatriates - referred to as migrant birds, Al-Kumur village as a collecting nest for classifications of nature and quarters, family names, Sawaqi (waterwheels), fertile muddy lands, and family divisions (Al-Alyab, Al-Doshab, Al-Kardab, Al-Zaidab, Al-Harymab, Al-Kromab, Al-Ardab, Al-Sanaga'h, Al-Sinaidab, Al-Assaseem, Al-Farhab, Al-Faraseen, Awald (sons of) Wad Maiyah, Awlad Al-Saem, Awlad Sha'r Al-Bal, Awlad Abdulqadir, Awlad Al-Huwar, and Awlad Wad Abu Sikeen.)

Names belong to natural elements. And there is a social and psychological effect in the affiliation, which is attracted to the life of the Nile, Desert or a blend of both.

6. Tales from Neighboring Villages

Every village has a name, every name has a tale, and every tale goes down to Souk Al-Kumur as prose, poetry, reality, imagination, or between reality and imagination. They spread from the informational forum to all neighboring villages, regions, and farther to distant cities.

Eleven villages formed a zone around Al-Kumur: Nasri Island, Fangol, Wedi Al-Qubah, Al-Azozab, Al-Ja'liyeen, Al-Jabrab, Al-Hawaweer, Galat Al-Bakriyah, Al-Tarjamiyah, Um Zor, Awald (sons of) Wad Al-Fadul Village.

There is also an abstract about Al-Biraiyab, their religious and Sufi impact on the region, and emergence of most of villages - or some of their inhabitants - from Nasri Island located on the part of the Nile that runs into

the Desert between the illusionary
longitudes and latitudes.

7. Composition of Al-Kumur's Population: Original and Immigrant Names

The extension of Al-Kumur Village between
the Nile and valleys defined affiliations of
names and populations, decoded symbols of
place, and acquired human being a social
dimension in time and place.

I mentioned three models of names: old ones
that originated from the Nile, immigrant
names that came with the advent of Islam,
and names that mimic nature.

The blend of names gave a new form of
language, meanings, and made a history that
affected the course of life and practices. The
effect of language got into the center of life
and development and gave a new thinking in
poetry, speech, and sarcasm – distributed in
other chapters.

There are also interventions of marriage and
impact of internal and external wars on the

migration of three tribes (Al-Shaygiyah, Al-Ja'liyeen, and Al-Hassaniyah) to Nasri Island.

As a result families were formed, extended, and mixed. They formed the present family fabric of Al-Kumur. Al-Kumur is one of the villages located on the west bank of the Nile between the 1st and 2nd cataracts with fringes on the edge of the Desert.

The British enhanced Al-Kumur's location by building a huge market regarded as the biggest market between Omdurman and Shandi anchorage. I dedicated a whole chapter for Souk Al-Kumur with its plans, commercial divisions, merchants, and peak of its social life especially the jokes of butchers and tales of merchants.

8. Tales and Popular Proverbs This is an important part in the Al-Kumur's social life. Due its importance and richness in information, I was forced to dedicate a special chapter for it. It helped me highlight works that took an influential collective shape in other communities such as the tale of Wad Abu Sikeen, the Lie Committee, and from women the tale of Al-Na'oom.

In this chapter I compiled all what is said: wisdoms, jokes, proverbs, daring characters related to jokes such as Ali Wad Jubarah, Abbas Wad Al-Hidai, Hamad Wad Rahamah, and Mohammed Ahmed Jubarah.

9. Compass of the Nile's Direction

This chapter deals with the meeting of the two Niles: the White and Blue, at the confluence and the preparation of the resulting Nile in making its way through the Desert that is not far away from the confluence where contours are diversified and changed. These are effects of a real war. Here begins the Nile's collision with the Desert and birth of the 1st cataract and emergence of two mountains: Al-Rawyan and Al-Atshan at Al-Hugnah Village.

The war made - from the region's contours - a natural compass that changed the Nile's current eastwards after it was running from south to north.

10. Between Reality and Fiction
This chapter contains three tales: African, Arabic, and Afro-Arab. The latter has a Sudanese character containing a mixture that formed the human being, eloquence of the natural language, and clarity of the Arab effect such as looking into the Desert with its manifestations, natural and intellectual dimensions, as well as the pillars, faith, and reality of the Islamic education. Here, I allowed the reader to go through the three tales that contain the truth, fancy, or something in between.

The imaginary tale represents the African fancy. It is the tale of Saleem. The second one is Fatima's (nicknamed Anez "goat" Al-Hambak). It represents something between reality and fiction. It embodies the Arab's eloquence and African imagination. In the third tale I included the marriage from jinn.

This chapter is an introduction to the Sudanese culture that combined facts of Arabism with the land of Africa.

11. Souk Al-Kumur

The number 11 in this chapter represents the two fingers when raised in the victory sign and indicates the sharing of the Nile and Desert culture in Souk Al-Kumur.

The Souk represents a social and informational forum which has its effect on the social, artistic, and literary life of the community of Al-Kumur, neighboring villages, and the region in general.

Beside commerce, the location of the Souk provided social services such as the intermingling of tribes and mixing of customs and traditions through interaction.

The commercial competition had also created an artistic line that represented the boom and progress for gaining the buyer, listener, and those standing by. Every one had his special art in presenting his commodity for gain and superiority.

The literary aspects e.g. poetry, tales, stories, and jokes, were also presented beside other material commodities, which created a competition in other aspects of life. In Souk Al-Kumur values of life including transactions and customs adhere and arts spread through media into neighboring village communities and distant places.

The Souk's interior sections are different from the exterior ones and each section is characterized by a different life. Outside the Souk there are the court building, Animals Market (livestock market) for Nile and Desert animals, the slaughterhouse for brokers and butchers, and house of Bint Zainaldeen for brewing liquors.

Each section of the inner Souk's squares has its characters and jokes such as butchers, merchants, vegetable sellers, farmers, barbers, blacksmiths, and tailors. Brokers are present in both sites, inside and outside the Souk.

The Souk's area is a place for showing customs, literary production, and commodities. People shop and select their needs. Meanings of social words spread in the Souk's space where words of language and wisdom, poetic contests, and narration of tales and stories in front of the cafes.

Poets depict Al-Kumur's nature and flourishing daily life in neighboring villages. They are the source of inspiration and eloquence in boasting, thanking, intimate discourse, lamenting, describing calamities, poetry contests, and love poetry about the Souk (market) that were usually sang in evening parties in the same day.

Al-Kumur's region is famous of female wailing poetry, as the rest of West Shandi Region. The shoppers respond to this poetry coming from neighboring village communities. Other types of poetry contests (imitating someone's poetry or competitions between two poets where each says two verses at a time) are also added and hence spread once again (such as the poem of Omar Girainat about the deceased Ahmed

Omar Nourallah). Topics of poetry as other things speak about the Nile or Desert.

In this chapter I dealt with problems of immigration, consequences, types of expatriates, and expatriate's points of view that changed from personal hopes to disgrace to the country.

Work and money is a comparison that combines the market, expatriation, and a show of other immigration objectives. Some hopes of expatriates changed into psychological problems that shock the feeling of patriotism within them and deprived them of the value of citizenship. Most of the separatists are expatriates.

Was the personal failure reflected on homeland? Or was it jointly shared between the interior and exterior? Or were these changes in the international community? Or were they the sum of all these causes together?

I tackled the problem of expatriates and immigration in an easy language of dialogue in Al-Nur's Café in Souk Al-Kumur with

Nile-Desert characters representing the Sudanese character to fend off the call for separation as I profoundly believe in the unity of Sudan.

I hope the language of dialogue has practically widened the topic of immigration. Comparing expatriates with types of birds is only a metaphor, but provides two spaces for the participation of the reader. The third space is dedicated for educational aspect of the academic curricula in the educational system, which instilled in generations the immigration concepts that led to the immigration of sentiments and departure of human beings.

The academic curricula, especially literary ones, have played a clear role in the period of immigration and modern Sudanese history. Geography moved us remotely from studying regions of Sudan such as Al-Angasana, Juba, and Sawakin. It brightened the picture of the external world and took us to Netherlands and Poland and made us cling to immigration.

The curricula and studies did not research the Nile River and courses of life between the Nile and Desert, but took us to Mississippi and Danube. And instead of climbing Jubal Marah, Sinkat, and Al-Atroon, we climbed the heights of Alps and Himalaya. We actually took an exhaustive and imaginative journey during school days to make friendships with children in Europe. We followed curricula and migrated. We ignored the friendship of Malwal, Bakri, Abaker, and Adarob. We were raised up to love the external world, aspire, and dream to see it.

The chapter also deals with Souk Al-Kumur and the diversity of jokes in the divisions of butchers, tailors, barbers, cafes, and old shops abounding in commodities on shelves, as well as examining books from Europe and India i.e. west and east.

12. The Nile is Taking and Offering
The Nile's offering is a blessing but its taking is evil in the journey between the

source and estuary. It pours blessings in Souk Al-Kumur. Haj Mohammed and his two sons, Sulaiman and Ali, come from the eastern side of the Souk; and Mohammed Wad Abdulraheem Siquair, comes from the west.

Sulaiman went to the source of the Nile and disappeared, but the Nile gave his brother Ali a lot. Thus is the Nile; it takes and gives. During the journey of Wad Abdulraheem to the market, he was attacked by a camel; had it not been for the Nile he waded in, he would have been killed by the camel.

This chapter shows the violence of the Desert with its dust, beauty, and the Nile's attack and retreat.

13. West of Souk Al-Kumur

West of the Souk (market) is characterized by dramatic life. There is the courthouse of the native administration, political leaders from Sheikhs of the Line (of villages) and Mayors, Animals Market, slaughterhouse, and house of Al-Hajah bint Zainaldeen.

Here, west of the market, knives cut animal throats and meat finds its way to the house of bint Zainaldeen.

14. Drama of Daily Life between the Cataracts

This chapter portrays the drama of daily events of a village between the cataracts of the River Nile in northern Sudan. The hot sun cools down during twilight and people meet at the River Nile. Playing in hot midday provides Desert's youths with strength. And between sadness and joy of children the stronger preys upon the weaker (survival of the fittest), and the march of generations does not stop.

Conclusion

Had the valleys form the natural desert gaps made and contributed in building the artificial gaps? And how valleys extended their deposits into the Nile in the form of sand and islands?

The conclusion shows how deserts and mountains form in the Nile; and how aquatic and amphibious animals follow desert sands and mountains into the Nile water. Tracking living things in Al-Kumur region - in land and water - has the nature of the Nile, Desert, and Mountain. They are indications to the Sudanese cultural affiliations

Chapter (1)
Al-Kumur and the Struggle of Nature

I write about Al-Kumur, as it is built in the region of natural struggle, between the Nile and the Desert. The Nile floods annually, overwhelms its basin, and covers sands. Valleys flow carrying sands from the Desert's heights to overflow the Nile basin. The area below Al-Kumur witnesses a battle between alluvium and sand. As a result Al-Kumur's land divides into the soil of the Nile and soil of the Desert.

The clear division of soil does not prevent it from advancing and mixing. The Nile floods with its armies to inundate the soil. Sands develop barricades so that Al-Kumur's region stands between the Nile's army and Desert's "Janjaweed" (a group of looters in Darfur's conflict in western Sudan).

The two soils mix and become red as clotted blood of many wars. They also become green and yellow. Sometimes only a thin thread separates between them from becoming sand or mud.

The battlefield is equally divided down the valley - from west to east - between the two giants into four names i.e. two for each. They are: Al-Karo and Abu Hawiyah, Um Bagarah, and Abu Jamal anchorage.

Chapter (2)
Geographical Nature of Al-Kumur

Al-Kumur is a colored piece of nature composed of plains, valleys, mountains, banks, streams, islands, different types of pebble plains, and vast areas of sands covered with white glittering stones and black rusty ones. It hides treasures and wealth of gold nuggets and ambergris underneath. Al-Kumur's land embodies secrets within it from ancient times.

Above this diverse nature there are square, rectangular, or circular mud buildings inhabited by tribes, clans, and families. Communities abound in jokes and sarcasm. Al-Sadah Mountains and the Desert extension of the noble Arab outstretch lie behind Al-Kumur. Below Al-Kumur flows the Nile - the old African spring – in this mulatto land composed of escarpments and Desert sands.

Why write about Al-Kumur? Because it is one of the villages of the cataracts, land of the buried history and treasures with monuments of ancient Sudan - from Al-Hugnah to Aswan. It is a region of the opposites where rocks pollinate water and the Nile quenches the thirst of the Desert.

Al-Kumur's land is a mixture of solid rocks, fresh water, and green banks where winds blow from the desert, and the breeze from upper Nile.

Water flows through time and generations. The Nile keeps washing the soil and faces of the beautiful girls of the Nile who unravel and interweave their hairs under the shady trees and clear water.

Girls divide their hairs into two front dangling braids glittering as the Desert sand and as a symbol of the Arabian east. They curl and interweave the rest intentionally as the Nile of Africa to their buttocks. Hanan throws the interwoven and scented hair onto Ahmed's face when dancing in an act titled "Shabal".

Summer is the season of crop harvesting and joys where wedding ceremonies, evening chats, and night games take place. Villages exchange congratulations on this occasion. People roam between villages on top of the mountains and deep valleys drumming "Dalookah" (a female Sudanese drum) and singing.

At night lamps are lit on these joyful occasions. Um Zor dances with Sadah and Fangol Mountains. From the edges of Abu Hawiyah valley come gazelles of Al-Bakiriyah and Al-Tarjamiyah. Um Sitrain sings in the end of the party" Oh amorous girl, the Kisrah (thin sheets of maize dough cooked on a hot baking tin) is good with Tagaliyah (dried shreds of meat, minced and cooked with onions, oil, spices, etc.), O, boy."

Here people laugh loudly and voices overwhelm the party, as they all know what Um Sitrain cunningly referring to. The gathering disperses and the night shrouds the village sited on the Nile bank calmly.

The night is more than cheerful, Al-Jabrab is blooming, Al-Azozab is fresher than fresh cool water, and Fangol is a cowry shell guarded by jinn snakes under the hooves and whinny of the British horses.

The British army came down from the Egyptian borders to Halfa region and Al-Khalifah (Caliph) Abdullah held a meeting for the Council of Princes in Omdurman for deliberations and viewpoints.

Prince Othman Dignah said: "Oh, Caliph of Al-Mahdi, I think we must never encounter the British army." Caliph replied:" How is that?" Prince Othman: "From now we have to move to old Halfa. On the way we have to incite village inhabitants not to interact with invaders and call them to join us in Jihad. We have to turn the battle into guerrilla warfare and distribute our men along the two banks of the Nile. We attack them in the dark and hide during the day. Thus Caliph, they fight an invisible army. Deprive them of sleep, convenience, and kill their soldiers along the way from Halfa to Omdurman. We try to steal their weapons and ordnance, because their weapons are better than ours. With our belief we protect our religion, land, and honor."

The British army camped on the top of Fangol Mountain and was overlooking Omdurman. You can see the villages west and east of the Nile within easy reach and below your feet.

Some British soldiers buried antiques they looted from Al-Barkal, Karimah, and old Nabata Kingdom in Fangol. Our bright past was buried to deny us seeing it. The difference was clear between our past and present where the British colonization drew a dividing line. As a result grandsons are backward thousands years from their forefathers. The forefather was buried, the glory was looted, and the grandson looked around and was in a loss.

Steamers sailed up the river loaded with heavy ordnance. Soldiers destroyed bastions and marched on the land of the Nile. One hundred and twenty kilometers only and this big army would arrive at Omdurman. The soldiers sang, while marching: "Omdurman here we come, Omdurman here we come."

The British army moved from its camp, on top of Fangol Mountain, towards Karari Mountains to confront the army of Caliph Abdullah Al-Ta'ishi. Queen Victoria was calling for the overthrow of Al-Mahadiyah rule. Souls and bodies of the dervishes under the patched jubbahs were overwhelmed with obedience and faith. They chanted: "Come on to Jihad. Come on to Jihad".

Omdurman at that time was the glory of Al-Mahadiyah and the capital of Sudan.

The day before the battle Prince Othman Dignah turned his back to Omudrman and headed east. He did not like the strategy of fighting. Had the Caliph listened to the advice of the Prince of the East, the history of Sudan and its modern face would have changed!

The preparation movement to face invaders was restless. Leader princes hoisted their flags and soldiers of Al-Mahahiyah quickly lined up under these big banners. Shouting and steps of soldiers rocked Omdurman. The Council of the Caliph met for the last time with the elite princes.

The battle of Karari started and the British army protected its back with the Nile and faced the Desert. Armies of Al-Mahadiyah were on the mountains. And from the top of Karari Mountains squads of the dervishes dashed as white eagles and charged the British army.

The artillery destroyed the Sudanese. Streams of blood came down the mountains. The banks of the Nile were swarmed with corpses. The war was over and the country entered an era of colonization where Omdurman was desecrated, proscribed, and graves were also dug up.

Fangol village could not be blamed. It committed no crime. Simply, it could not afford to fight the British army. There are some monuments still there in Fangol such as the stone-built camp which is called the "Enclosure of the Disbeliever." And some members of Al-Hassaniyah tribe are still there carrying their swords and knives under their arms.

Every year comes a grandson of one of the British soldiers with a map. He digs certain places in Fangol region, takes something, departs to Europe, and sells it in the international auctions or displays it in the European museums.

The British people departed rich to their country and left the looted Sudan. Sons of inhabitants of the Nile land followed suit and migrated.

Abu Sikeen: "immigration is like an eagle that snatches, pulls out feathers, and eats."

Abu Okaz: "expatriates are like a fish coming out of water. May Allah brings in oil and stops immigration for ever."

"Let us suppose that oil is discovered, do you think other nations will leave us enjoy it? God knows!"

Chapter (3)
The Nile's March and the Desert's Advancement

In the long eternal flow of the White Nile, it turns quietly as an old man to the meeting point (confluence) with the Blue Nile at Khartoum. And with the vigor of youth the Blue Nile rushes towards the confluence. They embrace each other and harmonize their procession between Al-Mawradah and Abu Roaf, where the great River Nile, heading north, is born.

The Nile prepares to go through the old Nubian Desert that opposed Abdullah bin Al-Sarah, the companion of Prophet Mohammed (PBUH). The Nile collides with the first parts of the Desert and produces the 1st cataract at Al-Rawyan and Al-Atshan Mountains, near Al-Hugnah village. Here the Nile leaves Al-Hugnah village to the west and changes its direction to the east.

The Desert advances from east to west, and the Nile from west to east. They adhere and other five cataracts are born.

Here is the epic of opposites. A thirsty desert from the depth of the Arabian Peninsula longs for water; and a Nile, springing from the wilderness of Africa, ready to quench the thirst of the desert.

A deep longing for meeting, shunning and coming together for fertilization, and down pouring cataracts in the murmuring water.

The Nile shifts and roams in its course between movements of sand and waves of the banks. The Nuba land rejoiced and turned green. Sand piled up as tents in the Nile paradise. New Desert and Nile tributaries were formed. Qahtan and Adnan (two main branches of the Arabs) tribes came along. Creeks and valleys branched.

Valleys came down into the Nile's course and with them came Al-Ja'liyeen, Al-Shaygiyah, and Al-Hassaniyah Arabs. Demoiselles landed and perched beside the

Bedouins. Sand grouses and spotted birds started to drink from the basins of the Arabs. The Arabs of the banks do not go deep into the Desert for cultivation. The Nile is within (a throw of a stone) easy reach. But nevertheless they yearn to practice the old Arab hobbies such as watching deers, smelling the countryside breeze, grazing sheep, singing Al-Dowbait (two-versed poetry) loudly, and sometimes cultivating their rain-irrigated lands in the Desert in seasons of the Nile's wrath and flood.

These people pat on the back of the Nile with Al-Seeja and Al-Taba games. They hold ceremonies when they rejoice; dance and delight when the Nile calms down. They take seeds and go deep into the Desert, which they inherited from their forefathers, tell tales proudly and insistently repeat that they are going to the old Nile's course!

They say this is the meeting point of the Nile and Desert. They battled here; and the land quivered and slanted to form the new Nile course. Farmers migrate annually, as the old Nile tribes do. Tribes migrated from the source and swamps of the canals, retreated from the estuary, and took the Nuba land as a pastureland.

These tribes built their temples and gathering places. Human beings and birds sang, branches of trees reeled, flutes played and mixed with human voices, and Kings sat on their thrones at Al-Hafir (water bore).

Chapter (4)
Al-Kumur and the Flood of Memories

Al-Kumur floods with memories! I have never thought that there is someone who loves Al-Kumur as much as I do. Throughout my life, I count the days eagerly to go back and live in it. I left Al-Kumur for elementary school and finished high school in Wadi Sayidna secondary school, a suburb north of Omdurman.

When I go back, in the school holidays, I used to spend all the day long playing with children in places I loved and dreamed of, between Abu Hawiyah valley and Souk Al-Kumur; and Al-Saqai sands and Al-Turki waterwheel.

I used to dream of swimming in Khor (gorge) Wad Al-Fadul, but my dreams change to Khor Mohyideen with our bodies covered with sand and mud.

In dreams we run and fall on the edge of Al-Tarad divider, built by the British during the colonization. Chasing in dreams is a fearful thing. When I wake up I thank Allah that the dreams are not real and I go back to sleep once again.

During school holidays, I used to visit places of my dreams and childhood. I was then not more than twelve years old. I could not believe that I was in Al-Kumur again, playing, running, and living with my peers Mustafa Abdulseed, Awad Al-Asad Karoam, and Al-Tigani Umbokol.

Twenty five years are the sum of my immigration. They took me away of Al-Kumur, but did not take Al-Kumur out of my soul. I left Al-Kumur for education and later for work. I used not to come back except in holidays; insisting to live in Al-Kumur reluctantly.

At the end of the holiday, I sadly fall back into immigration, whether inside the Sudan, neighboring country – in the Arabian Gulf region, or the first world - USA.

I wept during the days of expatriation inside the Sudan or the Gulf region. But when I left for other countries I even wept more for the past days.

That village is amazing. There is a yawing gap between us. I sit on the edge of the gap and it is on the opposite side. We collaborate to bridge the gap during holidays, but when I leave it widens once more.

I have actually dreamed of falling in a deep hole. The sore reality of departure wakes me up. And thus days slip as sand in an hourglass and once more I am drifted far away, to the unknown of expatriation. I do not know where my destination or footsteps will lead me to, or for how long! Many times I thought of Al-Kumur's soil before going to bed. My dreams extend, during sleep and expatriation. I wake up and the beloved soil is not there.

Many times I hoped for the big dusty courtyard with its many sand-penetrated doors and other doors overlooking the Nile.

I suddenly wake up and find myself in the workplace away of homeland.

I still think of my peers, who never left Al-Kumur, playing with a mixture of sand and mud, exposed to the blowing warm air, Nile breeze, and walking on red, black, and white stones.

Hamad: "we stay here and guard Al-Kumur's dust and colored stones. You go away, educate yourselves and come back."

Al-Sir: "I guard Al-Kumur and these white stones."

Hamad:" our stones are white gold. Have you ever heard of white gold?"

Al-Sir: "we know the desert-colored yellow gold."

Hamad: "but listen! The white gold is for the white people and the yellow for the yellow people."

Al-Sir: "do you mean the black people have nothing!"

Hamad: "they have the black gold."

Al-Sir: "Is there a black gold?"

Hamad: "Yes, the oil."

Al-Sir: "we have neither white nor black gold. We have the Nile blue color. Oh beautiful, we love the Nile." He raises his hand to avoid a blow from Hamad.

They went to swim. Al-Sir took off his clothes, retreated and ran naked, dived into the Nile, and dipped. We thought he will not come up again. When he came up he said:" curse the oil!"

Al-Sir: "O, people listen. We have neither the black nor white. We have the blue color with the yellow color, the color of the Desert, what does they make?

They all shouted: "the green color."

Al-Sir: "Aha, we are the green blessed people; say Amen."

We run, after the flood season is over, on dusty, cracked, and dry soil with its sides up that sounds like a dry fodder when you walk on it. We play with it and laugh. We used to play and tour the Nile and Desert.

Mustafa Abdulseed, from Al-Hassaniyah tribe, fair-colored, fond of razing hunting dogs, and perfects Al-Seeja game, is always thirsty and longing to the Nile. He married a Nilotic lady from the Nuba Mountains, and was blessed with a number of boys and girls. He came back with them to his folks in Al-Kumur. When he greets you he used to say: "Hello, Hello Allah has brought you. Hey, man you went far away! Come on, sit down."

Awad Al-Asad, were born in the nearest village homes to the Nile. He perfects Al-Tab game. Whenever he meets Mustafa, they wrestle with hands and words. He is a Nilotic who loves Nasri Island and yearns to the Arab customs. He married his cousin and was blessed with a number of boys and girls. He never misses an occasion in Al-Kumur. When he greets you he used to say:" How are you? Hey man, are you going back again? Seize expatriation. It is enough. Please, sit down."

Al-Tigani Umbokol, named Sufi and his grandfather is named after a village built beside the Nile near the farms. When he meets Mustafa, their voices go down in a conversation as a token of appreciation and love. His voice goes up in a normal speech or when playing around beyond the limit of courtesy. When he meets Awad Al-Asad, they understand each other and make a team in playing cards.

Abdullah and Tigani - both natives of Umbokol - brought up with an intrinsic hate to country side hunting with Mustafa or going down the Nile with Awad Al-Asad. They acquired the knowledge of the two cultures from books. They master English, Arabic calligraphy, arts of courtesy and speech, and play on musical instruments. They welcome you by saying: "you arrived welcomingly in the Nile and settled welcomingly in the Desert". Expatriation is somewhat not bad, in cases of urgent need, but must be temporary. Please, sit down."

I sat down with the big poet Mohammdannh Al-Jahoori in Omdurman. I told him about what was previously mentioned in the past pages. I told him about the yearning and longing to Al-Kumur.

He said to me: "thank Allah for coming back. Aha, when are you going back to Al-Kumur?" I told him: "Oh, man, if not tomorrow, it will be after tomorrow." I told him the story of my long traveling which took me away of Al-Kumur while I was fighting to come back.

Al-Jahoori said: "I don't know how you tolerate disunion! Hey man, I stayed in Khartoum one week only with Brigadier Al-Tayyeb Ahmed Mohammed Khair and I wrote this poem titled (Yearn to Al-Kumur)."

The poem reads:

"Oh, how I long to the distant Al-Kumur. My affection is blazing.

Oh, how I long to Abdo, Fatah, and his (maternal) uncle Saeed in the shop.

Oh, how I long to my mother, father, Rahmah, and the unique star.

I am to my felicity and that Safiyah. Oh, Lotfi seeing your son is the Eid (feast).

It is impossible for me to sleep in the night. I stay awake calling the distant star.

I ask the looming moon about Nasri Island and the tiered palm trees.

They say to me if you long for Kumur go and leave the promises and the Brigadier.

I do not answer someone who is hard-hearted towards his country and his beloved home.

And weep for him with tears of repentance, but how my tears could be useful.

In the end I send greetings to Al-Turki, the Quranic wooden board, and Quran memorizing groups in the Mosque.

To everyone asking about me, I extend my sincere greetings and love.

I am already sitting on embers, for I never love the spot (Omdurman).

Soon I will see you Kumur, Oh, Nasri laugh a lot for me."

This poem is an expression of affection of five days only away from (home) Al-Kumur. What do you think about twenty five years in expatriation!!

Al-Kumur acquired from nature the diversification; the lofty mountains, deep valleys, vast plains, and the great Nile flowing in the middle of Al-Kumur. Mountains of Fangol, Al-Sadah, rising agricultural lands of Magboul, in addition to Khor (gorge) Mohyideen, Khoy, escarpment, and Wedy (small valley).

All these symbols meet below Al-Kumur, unite with the Desert, Nile course, and deluge. Here appear the Arab features of Africa above the surface with two facts every year – desertification and inundation.

Around Al-Kumur tributaries go down with rain water into the valley below the Souk (market) and from there to the Nile's course. At the end of Abu Hawiyah valley in Khor Mohyideen, the desert sand covers a big part of the muddy land; and the Nile floods with mud to cover the sand.

Weapons of sand and mud spread on the public square of Al-Kumur. They collide and unite since the beginning of creation. Valleys flow rapidly with floods like edges of swords to cover Al-Kumur's land with mud. Nile waves surge to thrust fleeing sand and fold it.

Between spears and blades of swords Al-Kumur shouts and calls "I am Al-Khumrah (Sudanese female fragrance composed of many perfumes left in a bottle for some days to ferment) from the oysters of the sea (Nile) and Al-Mahraibah (aromatic plant) from the Mountain's chest."

Inhabitants move to calm down the dispute. They hold meetings inside their houses, discuss matters - sometimes loudly or quietly – look for a way to satisfy the Nile and the Desert and reconcile the dispute.

Inhabitants built bridges and dams. The British interfered and built Al-Tarad divider – a lofty road above the surface of the Nile and Al-Karo that separates between them, which inhabitants use during floods. It starts from the sandy valley below Souk Al-Kumur. It winds inside Al-Karo heading westwards and south west to villages of Wad (son of) Keer, Wad Al-Habashi (Abyssinian), Wad Hamid, and Sawarid.

Sands do not head for the above mentioned villages only, but they head as usual to west and south of Sudan. As a result, Al-Tarad screen became an artificial desert gap.

Al-Kumur ended the dispute by more unification, quenched the thirst of the Desert, dispersed pearls of the Arabic language as boats on the water surface, and customs spread on the green banks.

The natives reached an agreement to satisfy the two sides by leading life on both the Nile and the Desert. They sometimes side with the Nile, cultivate its lands and in other times with the Desert. They enjoy the blessings of cultivation and crop after the hard work.

They cultivate the Desert once and lands of the Nile twice. They cultivate and harvest both sites so that Al-Kumur could become an Afro-Arab topography combining the two colors.

The meeting of the thirsty Desert with the Nile was a yearning to the flow of water deep into the Desert. They faded away in a long cuddling and then flew into the new course. From that time, grandchildren still track the road of yearning and meeting place to fulfill practices of life by cultivating lands of the Nile and Desert.

Natives of Al-Kumur who traveled were usually attracted to the struggle field. They try not to miss a single episode. They ask when they come back: "Aha how is the Nile and rain?"

Abu Hawiyah valley descends with storm floods. People queue up on its banks looking Al-Sayyal and Al-Salam (acacia) trees which it uproots. They are its weapon in beating the mud and threatening the Nile, as it deems that it will win the battle. People applaud; their fears disappear and see a good omen in cultivating their rural lands.

The Nile's color changes into dusty. It floods calmly and brimful with a suppressed latent anger. It responds to the natives and pleasant neighbors by overwhelming the valleys. For two months, the land on the range of vision is flooded. The water of rage and lust leaks inside the earth. The Nile then calms down, rubs the chest of the land while retreating to its course leaving behind wet sand that grows plants and fills udders.

People sing two songs for harvest and joy. Whenever tow natives meet they hold a contest for two-versed poems, rhymed prose, and sweet words about marriage and circumcision. Al-Kumur's nights flame with joys and the market abounds with blessings of harvest.

After harvest, the people of Al-Kumur relax and a wide leisure time prevails. They enjoy playing and night chatting. They divide into two groups: a group that plays Al-Seeja and hunt with dogs and the other plays Al-Tab.

Al-Seeja Game

People make circles around Al-Seeja game and divide into groups, camps, and teams. Tools of Al-Seeja are twenty five holes in the ground and two different color pebbles: cores of dates and lime stones called (dogs) that chase each other. Al-Seeja dogs represent the Desert.

The match starts with chasing and words such: chase the dog, catch the rabbit, and which way your game is going to escape? Al-Seeja vocabulary and tools came down from the Desert. Al-Seeja leaders are Al-Hadi, Wad Qasimalseed, Siddiq, Othman, and Wad Abbas; Arab names or classified as such.

Al-Tab Game

Tools of Al-Tab game are the branches of palm trees. One side is peeled off to be different from the green one. Thus branches symbolize the Nile and Desert. The vocabulary and tools of the game have Nilotic and Desert meanings. Everyone plays to access his mother into paradise. Mother will not access paradise unless the four Tabas fall and their (white) interior is facing upwards. It is a symbol of the Arabs. All mothers are chased with an evil creature called Al-Kokaraj, which prevents mothers from accessing paradise. Victories are by crossing the sea (in Sudan sometimes the Nile is referred to as the sea) and access paradise.

The famous players of Al-Tab are: Ali Wad Siddiq, Hamad Wad Rahamah, Mohammed Wad Jubarah, and all Al-Faraseen (the Nilotic group that migrated from Nasri Island.)

Before playing, wrangling, challenges, hand twisting, and show of power start. Ali Wad Siddiq says: "cut the branches of palm trees (stripped off their leaves)." One of them unsheathe his knife and after challengingly staring at them, he cuts the branch and tries to hit one of them as a gesture of going too far in the challenge.

The length of the branch is six inches. The others prepare the game field, which includes the finishing line, the sea (Nile), and paradise. The terms of the game are divided between the Nile and Desert; as palm trees grow beside the Nile and oases.

Hamad Wad Rahamah starts with two Tabas in each hand and throws them in the air. The four Tabas come down gradually with a systematic sound that resembles the trot of hooves of a horse about to stop. All await the result, which takes one of five possibilities: 1. Al-Taba, 2. Telli, 3. Day, 4. Sta', 5. or Arabs.

Explaining Al-Taba Game

Statistics in Al-Taba game has many possibilities. The four Tabas, with their colors - green and white -form five possibilities: three green and one white called Al-Taba; one green and three white called Telli; two white and two green called Day; four green called Sta'; and four white: called Arabs.

Importance of Possibilities in the Two Games

Sta' is the first step, which is exiting (departing) the finish line. Al-Taba is for crossing the sea (Nile). Arabs is for accessing paradise. The rest of possibilities are used for forward or backward movements.

The movement of mother and race start. Sta' is six steps. The white i.e. exactly the opposite direction, means Arabs and means four steps. Those two steps mean the Nile and Desert. If winning the game required six steps, then the green color is required. At that moment they shout: "Paradise, Paradise; Island, Island".

Survival requires four points. Then Arabs is required. When throwing the branch of the palm tree they call (Arbab Dar Bana); means "I see the door of our fathers' home" i.e. paradise, Islam, or yearning to their homeland they left in the Arabian Peninsula. There are many possibilities in the Desert Al-Seeja game with its lime stones, which are eaten by pregnant women during Waham (carving for some food during pregnancy). Some women eat the Nile mud so that the baby girl takes a Nilotic color – colors from yellow to blue to twin between the Arab and African lands.

If the symbol was Telli, which means figure three, they say:" Telli stood up and descended i.e. headed towards the Nile."

To show features of nature and color in Sudan, here people describe the black man as "a green man" – a mixture of yellow and blue – an expression to the meeting of the Nile and Desert. They do not describe a person as black! They say: "he is blue colored." They relate him to the Nile water. They describe a fair colored person as "a yellow man" and relate him to the Desert.

Nilotics favor Al-Taba game and the Desert people Al-Seeja game.

The geographical nature of Al-Kumur is equally divided between the Nile and Desert. Below Al-Kumur, from west to east, there are four main sections: Al-Karo, Abu Hawiyah valley, Um Bagarah, and Abu Jamal anchorage.

Al-Karo is the muddy land, Hawiyah is the camel's saddle, Bagarah is the cow – animal of the Nile and Jamel (camel) is the Desert's ship.

Al-Kumur is built in the landscape between the Nile and Desert. Houses are built of a mixture of the two soils – sand and mud – and roofs are hoisted above the valleys as castles. Eyes (ports) opened in room walls high up the buildings, overlooking the roofs and vast Desert space. Other ports are down below and overlook the green land of the Nile.

The courtyards widened and windows installed in the middle of walls. Every house has a verandah with two doors opening on two directions so that air and dust – yellow and blue – can access.

Two adjacent seasons of floods: rain storms and River Nile. Inhabitants stand on the edge of the valley encouraging the flow of water by applauding, screaming, yelling, and kidding that resembles the cheering of Al-Seeja and Al-Taba contests.

Rain storms precede the Nile flood. The fine sand comes in June and July. But the Nile floods in August and September – fifteen days later – to beat the valleys.

The features of nature in Al-Kumur are clear in forms and divisions of houses. Behind buildings the sight is lost in the Desert horizons with its historical and social dimensions, deep in the Empty Quarter and teachings of heavenly religions in the Arabian Peninsula. But if you look at the Nile, you will sail with imaginations of Africa and depths of the lakes.

Anciently, house doors were opened towards the Nile as they believed in it. But after the advent of Islam, the verandah is provided with two doors – one towards the Nile and the other towards the Qiblah (direction of Kaaba – the Holy Mosque in Makkah).

This knowledge is formed and added to the Sudanese heritage. There are also cultures that run in the opposite direction, which came from Rome, Athens, and rest of Europe.

Down Al-Kumur is abounding in sports: physical exercises, football matches, festivals, Sudanese and Arab camel race, as well as performance of Eid prayers. There are also horse races, swimming, and mobilization of people for harvest of crops where drums are beaten and the procession heads towards the Nile. Beautiful girls keep singing:

"Our bridegroom arrived at the sea (Nile) and tonight he will proceed to his bride. He has cut branches of palm trees; tonight he will proceed to his bride."

Al-Karo is part of the Nile where sand deposited on its edges to separate it. The Nile sees this as a transgression and challenge. As a result it floods every year and carries alluvium to recover its Al-Karo. Between the attack of the Nile and retreat of the sand, mountains erode. This nature inspired the poet Al-Jahoori to say:

"With the scent of alluvium, the Nile surged over Al-Karad (a dry muddy soil)."

"At the scent of a distant rain, the Nile escaped (retreated)."

These verses are indication to the struggle of the Nile and valleys. In the latter verse the scent of a distant rain comes as a result of rains and expected rain storms in the tributaries and valleys heading towards the Nile. Before the escape, the Nile surged over Al-Karad.

These poetic verses spread the distinct smell of a distant rain and Nile alluvium, heralding the uproar of the Desert armies and rain storms.

Of the landmarks built by the British in Al-Kumur's region, is Al-Tarad (divider) road to keep water inside the basin. Wad Hamid, the agriculturalist, separates Al-Karo from the Nile. Thus the Nile is offended. It roars and floods.

The body of Al-Tarad starts from the valley sand in Al-Kumur and heads southwards to parallel the Nile as a sand stream in the opposite direction of the water.

Al-Tarad is an artificial gap and Abu Hawiyah valley is a natural gap composed of sand valleys that pour into the Nile and appear as desert islands in the summer seasons. Al-Tarad enters Al-Karo from east and sands follow it as a southern caravan crossing the African lands. Thus nature changes the camel-razing Arabs into Bagarah (cowboys) and Hamar (a tribe in western Sudan) into shepherds of sheep and camels.

The rivers are also named in Arabic e.g. Bahr Al-Arab (Arab Sea (river)) and Bahr Al-Gazelle (Al-Gazelle Sea (river)) in the land of Sudan.

The flood is over and winter crops are cultivated. Winter fades away and summer advents. The Nile water is clear again, and the day is hot with mirages and sweat.

The farmer tightens his belt on his waist and prepares himself for the summer cultivation. The period of the summer crops is long, but onion has the longest. Onion stays in the ground approximately for six months. It is the most productive and exhausting crop; and the least profitable due to difficulty of storage and cost of transport.

Farmers sell onion cheap (with whatever price, as they say) to avoid its deterioration. They always curse its cultivation, because it exhausts their bending bodies over pickaxes under the searing heat and laborious work.

Merchants go down to the villages during harvest days and set their traps and conical straw houses (onion storehouses). When restaurants of the Capital Khartoum consume the onion, its price hikes and trigger trucks to carry it to the capital city. When the lights of Omdurman loom in the horizon, travelers congratulate each other for the safe arrival, though profits go to the pockets of merchants.

Merchants advance towards the villages in the next season and the villages advance towards the Nile. The dispersed rooms resemble the rocks of the cataracts coming out in the middle of the water where waves penetrate these rocks and come out roaring. It is the tale of the eternal Nile and the long journey.

Sweet water explodes around solid bodies of cataracts irrigating crops and shrouds cores of dates with pellicles. The Nile irrigates date palms to produce different kinds of dates e.g. Al-Ajwah (pressed dates) and Al-Gindail.

Life cycle goes on every year. Birds come and go. The banks swarm with movement, shouting, noise, jokes, and songs. Steamers depart and anchor. Youths come out leaping off the boats. Women come along with milk. Old men cross Al-Jamam (gradually accumulating water) mud and resist the desertification and Al-Haddam (falling of the bank edges into the Nile). Musical tones are played on the river bank, between nature and human beings.

Chapter (5)
Social Life in Al-Kumur

There are eleven villages around Al-Kumur in a circular shape. Al-Kumur appears in the middle as the center of the circle. Social life of inhabitants is related to kinship, knowledge, and cooperation. In Al-Kumur there is an interest in naming houses, waterwheels, and muddy fertile lands by relating them to forefathers.

Resident families in Al-Kumur are: Al-Alyab, Al-Doshab, Al-Kardab, Al-Hiraimab, Al-Zaidab, Al-Ardab, Al-Sanaqah, Al-Sinaidab, Al-Asoomab, Al-Kromab, Awlad (sons of) Wad Maiyah, Awlad (sons of) Al-Sa'em, Awlad (sons of) Sha'r Al-Bal, Awlad Abdulqadir, Awlad Al-Huwar, and Awlad Wad Abu Sikeen.

In the neighboring villages there are similar sections most of them grew in Nasri Island, one of ten following villages neighboring Al-Kumur: Nasri, Fangol, Wedi Al-Qubah, Al-Azozab, Al-Ja'leen, Al-Jabrab, Al-

Hawaweer, Al-Qalah, Al-Tarjamiyah, Um Zor, and Awlad Wad Al-Fadul.

Al-Kumur is the urban center of these villages as it contains the Souk (market), court, bus and other commercial vehicles parking lots, schools, and polyclinics; in addition to its proximity to the Nile and agricultural lands.

Many types of birds hover about the agricultural production and come down to pick seeds and other blessings. Other domestic birds swarm around among the people e.g. pigeons, native and (veterinary) hens, turkeys, and other easily frightened birds such as ducks and geese, and wild ones such as vultures and eagles. There are also the hunted birds which distant themselves carefully such as the colored and smooth "birds of heaven", Wad Abraq, and Um Qairadoon (Desert peacock) which runs for short distances and suddenly stops raises its tail, swaggers, and looks around.

Some birds live inside the houses, convey talks, and whisper; others spend the whole day flying between the houses and market. Some birds travel for short distances; others travel abroad to the Persian Gulf region and other remote places.

Four characters weave Al-Kumur's threads of life in the social and political occasions. They are Hamad Wad (son of) Rahamah, Mohammed Ahmed Wad Jubarah, and Saeed Wad Salim. They understand economics; stand up for market discussions, crop prices, and seeds. They focus on election seasons; the candidate program and his tribe. They tour the inside rings of tambourines beaten in praise of Prophet Mohammed (PBUH). Nevertheless, they attend parties that include Al-Ardah (show of manhood) and Shabal (girls throwing their braided and scented hair into their faces). They drink tea voraciously and do not stop drinking coffee, cigarettes, and snuff.

They also host strange people and treat them with generosity, solve female teachers' housing problems, transference of teachers, attend meetings of parents' council in schools, collect donations for the health center, burry the dead, and receive condolences. They give themselves the right of intervention in who will lead prayers (Imam) in the mosque and Eid sermon.

Hamad Wad Rahamah says to his group: "Hey, guys, there is no water for two days. The pump is out of order. What do we do?"

Ali Wad Siddiq says: "the pump will not click unless we collect money to repair it."

Mohammed Wad Jubarah: "What about the money we have collected in the Souk (market) of last Thursday, have we spent it?

Hamad Wad Rahamah:" not a penny is left."

Saeed Wad Salim:" Aha, now I tell you that we have to wake up tomorrow early and start collecting money. We have to start with the down village, for these days expatriates are in the country. We have to hurry up before they spend their money."

They all agreed to take breakfast in Al-Nur's Restaurant and Café; and afterwards they start the tour of money collection.

Every day before Maghrib (dusk) prayer, the big four resolve the problem of the water pump for tomorrow, electric generator for the lighting, and make sure that playing cards are available in Dar Al-Kateebah (home of the battalion).

They have recruited eyes from the lower generation who know about those entering and exiting Al-Kumur, departing tomorrow, and emigrating. They know the banquets, parties, and invitees at the edge of the village. They go without invitation, inspect and farewell departing people, and receive the arrivals.

Village youths combine between generosity, self-denial, joke, and sarcasm. They address generations below and above them with different languages and jest with the young.

The generation below them such as Ali Wad Jubarah, Abbas Wad Al-Hidai, Wad Abu Sikeen, Hamad Wad Abdulraheem, Fathalrahman, and Wad Sha'r Al-Bal who always reiterates: "we are the village cocks and they will not jail us for peeping."

Wad Abraq hovered about and landed. It flew for a short distance to near the she-birds (girls) of Wad Abraq. Suso turned around, chirped, leapt twice, and fell on its wife. Um Qairadoon was watching. Varieties of birds that do not constantly live in Al-Kumur or abandon it, but hover about between Al-Kumur and cities of the Three-Towns Capital Khartoum (Omdurman, Khartoum North, and Khartoum).

Some birds maneuver during Eid (the Lesser of Greater Bairam) prayers around the people wearing the snow-white garments and turbans. These birds stay away for one year. Some birds come during school holidays and others during weekends. They love loitering around in Al-Kumur and regret the short hours of weekend – Thursday and Friday.

Wad Abraq tours the market landing on top of the verandah pillars. It builds its nests and hides its young. It is a mean bird. It eavesdrops and hears secrets of people, turns its head right and left with turns of talk from one man to the other, scratches under its tail with its beak, becomes restless, and amazed of sons of Adam. It says:" the son of Adam has two legs as me. They set traps to each other and backbite, but they agree upon me. Their young twist dry branches of palm trees where my nest is and drop my young to play with them.

During Friday prayer, Wad Abraq chirps in the corners of the mosque. One prayer turns to it and says: "May Allah harm this sparrow." Another man responds to him by saying:" hey man, this sparrow will neither leave us to pray nor hear the sermon." Another says: "is the weekend – Thursday and Friday – not over so that it can fly away and leave us?" Hamad Wad Rahamah: "I swear by Allah, whenever it comes to Al-Kumur, we are in the preaching and guidance and it is in bad deeds." Mohammed Ahmed Jubarah: "Hey brother, please abandon us." Saeed Wad Salim, who rubs his forehead restlessly and turning his face to the ground: "Please, get lost brother!" Hamad Wad Rahamah: "please listen to me pals. Stand up and congratulations for the Eid (feast)." He stands up and the rest of them follow suit.

The preacher finds himself standing alone. He wonders, laughs, and finishes his speech fast to avoid embarrassment. He gets in the bus which heads westward to Omdurman while keeping some utterance to himself.

Some people call the colored smooth birds "Heaven's Birds". They come from Hijaz (Makkah region) and spread in Al-Kumur in the rainy season and during valley floods. The Nile alluvium contaminates expatriates' white clothes and they usually refrain from cultivation.

They are accustomed to sands, countryside, and reiterate Persian Gulf songs especially the song of singer Mayhed Hamad who says: "I love the countryside and the beautiful girl. I love the Bedouins and homelands. I love you before your kinfolks and mine, or neighbors know."

When the Nile floods and its water lodge remote banks, it gradually calms down brimful. After it retreats the muddy lands crack and small insects come out. "Heaven's Birds" feed on them.

People speak about the tasty food in Al-Kumur and why food is different and not tasty in countries of expatriation! For the Nile water is sweet and the land is fertile – a mixture of mud and sand. Al-Honaiter seeds when planted, they grow and bear leaves that can be cooked. How delicious is Okra with beaten Sabaroq (leaves of the cowpea plant) and mutton from Abbas Wad Al-Haj, Sheikh of the butchers. It has no match even in the famous Lebanese "Ya Mal Al-Sham" restaurants.

"Heaven's Birds" are amusing. They do not stay long in Al-Kumur. They start their journey back when the Nile goes down and vault waters flow from Al-Karo to the Nile.

They all start procedures of the journey fast as they are afraid of taxes imposed on expatriates and paying costs for the cultivating family lands. How many do the father and (maternal and paternal) uncle's demand? How much is the cost of seeds, grading, leveling, plowing, and planting seeds? I tell you, it is better to depart.

When the space swallows the Boeing aircraft, "Heaven's Birds" disappear from Al-Kumur. People keep on remembering the happy occasions. For during the vacation betrothals are accomplished, some youths get married, others are even blessed with children. Many youths living in the charitable societies and bachelors' houses dream happily.

Life returns to its usual tempo in Al-Kumur after the post office frequent letters of expatriates. Correspondences, greetings, calls, yearning, predictions, promises, denials, ambitions, backbiting, and curses are all behind (other side of) the Red Sea.

Hamad Wad Rahamah says: "I swear by Allah, expatriates' utterance is high behind the Sea."

Mohammed Wad Jubarah: "hey man, by Allah, their utterance is like the utterance of Abu Tee Tee (echo)."

"I think your pal has received a remittance."

"Did you hear of the money?"

"Yes."

"But he kept silent completely, and not a word about them!"

"Wait tomorrow we will be with him."

Saeed Wad Salim: "hey Ali Wad Siddiq, Babekir Badri; Hamad Wad Rahamah is speaking."

The fourth kind of birds is rare and its period -between the fall of the Nile and cultivation – is short when the basin of Wad Hamid is full of mud, not devoid of canals, and linked gorges that narrow and widen - as galaxies with radiant planets - come down.

Water begins to discontinue and canals dry up heralding the end of the flood season. The thin white long-legged cow birds appear and spread their wings. They come form unknown world and signal the end of a year. They lead rough routes and tracks in migration from distant and mysterious places.

The natives of Al-Kumur know the time when the cow birds visit them infrequently, but they do not know locations of their nests and when they lay and hatch their eggs. They come with their young birds chirping in early morning and forenoon. They know the migration route and appear at intervals below Al-Kumur's valley.

They give the false impression that they are leaving eastward and deep in the air their leader, which is at the tip of the semi triangular shape of the migrant birds, changes its direction westwards – where our Nile comes from.

With a temporary content and incomplete conviction all generations stay in state of migration. All the generation will be in a state of migration till the cold south wind blows, treaties are signed, and the war in southern Sudan is over.

Story of Mahmoud Wad Mayyah

Mahmoud saw a corpse floating on the Nile, grabbed it and went to see Busharah, mayor of Al-Kumur, who ordered him to cover it and inform the police station in Wad Al-Habashi, which is twelve kilometers away. Mohamoud left every thing behind and went to inform the police station and was subjected to many questions. He returned back and was ordered to burry it.

Mahmoud mobilized the men and buried the corpse. He undoubtedly won a great reward from Allah, but lost his work that sustains his family. He came back cursing the day he saw the corpse.

Less than a week, and when he went down to tie the boat, he saw another corpse. He stood and remembered what had happened to him previously. He was holding a long stick for pushing the boat away from the bank. With that stick he pushed the corpse into the Nile. He said: "go ahead may Allah make things easy for you. Shandi police station and Al-Damer Directorate are ahead."

Mahmoud pushed the corpse and looked at it. It turned itself around due to the strong current and headed eastwards. He muttered:" let go of it Mahmoud. Are you looking for troubles?"

Once again a third corpse was floating on the Nile. Mahmoud and Mohammed Wad Abdulsamad were eating a Sudanese Kisrah with tomatoes under a palm tree beside the Nile.

Mahammed Abdulsamad shouted: "uncle Mahmoud, stand up!"

Mahmoud: "where to?"

Mahammed: "there is a floating corpse."

Mahmoud: "hey man, go on eating." He further added: "the corpse passed through Al-Kalaklat, Khartoum, and Abu Roaf where people eat cooked food, meat, and fats and they did not see it. How come that you, who eats with water, saw it?"

Mahmoud directing his speech to Abdulsamad: "let it go. Police stations and the Directorate are ahead!"

They laughed and continued eating. They continued their life and the corpse went to an unknown world. How many strayed men and animals died in the Desert and a drowned man's corpse floated on waves!!

Story of Al-Nuwairi with Education and Al-Faki's Khalwah

A Khalwah (a religious school for memorizing Holy Quran and teaching Arabic language) was opened in Nasri Island. Children were brought to it. Al-Nuwairi refused to go to this school. He used to spend all the day long away from home fearing Al-Faki (a religious teacher who memorizes children verses of the Holy Quran and teaches Arabic language).

After many procedures and tricks Al-Nuwairi was finally led to Al-Khalwah. He used to keep silent in one of the corners. Al-Faki used all means that ranged from sweet words, presents, and beating to incite him. But all these means were useless and futile and his pupil Al-Nuwairi never uttered a word. For two weeks, he was only looking at the teacher. He was sent in a vacation for one week. He came back and nothing changed.

Al-Faki: "you Nuwairi, are you originally from here or came from somewhere else?

Al-Nuwairi: "I am from Nasri Island."

Al-Faki: "say in the name of Allah most Gracious, and most Merciful." Al-Nuwairi stared at Al-Faki and said: "but you will not stop at it."

From that day his father took him to work in the Nile boats. He went to learn from the Nile!

Al-Nuwairi met Wad Maiyah; two boatmen (one original and the other is a migrant) on the Nile sailing between Nasri Island and Al-Kumur.

Khalawi and Divans

Each family or neighboring group in Al-Kumur has a big building known as Al-Khalwah or divan (a gathering place) where big occasions are held, guest are honored, and travelers are lodged. Here people take their breakfast in the holy month of Ramadan (fasting), Eids (Lesser and Greater Bairams), and perform prayers and hold meetings.

In front of each divan or Khalwah there are a number of big water jars to cool water. Al-Khalwah contains beds, straw mats, and ewers.

The natives inspect Al-Khalwah in the morning and evening. He who sees a guest must inform the neighbors to participate in hosting him. Al-Khalawi (plural of Al-Khalwah) and divans are social edifices as Africa that has endless blessings.

In Al-Khalawi there are also councils for Islamic sciences, rings to memorize Holy Quran, answer questions of jurisprudence, marriage, and divorce. They represent the flood of Africa and Arab advancement. The young learn in Al-Khalwah the good listening and basics of reading and writing.

Writing is a cause for visiting Al-Kumur, enter Al-Khalawi and divans, sit on the village soil, walk in a narrow street or winding alleys, speak and laugh with people I know, hear the whistling of the dusty wind and rustling of trees, bleating of goats, and buzzing of hornets. Writing has made me hear all these sounds which I miss them a lot.

I imagine the frigid time in early morning when cells of laziness and activity stretch themselves. Slow time contains few things and a lot of contemplation. Following that is yawning, sighs, cheering, sweeping, and a lady's hoarse voice calling her neighbor for something.

"Did you hear the news?"

"The one you have seen and heard!!"

"We have heard and may Allah save us! I will tell you later!!"

"Aha, the wind started to blow."

She did not wait for an answer from her neighbor and got down off the separating wall.

The lantern fell down, sheet iron whirled, trays flew up, cans hit each other, and utensils and vessels clamored. "Get inside fast the dusty wind has blown". The soil was shaken off, pillows were wrapped up, and bedcovers were collected.

"We dusted off 'evil and heat'! Get up boy and shake off the dust."

"Mother, where is my brother Bakheet?"

She craned her neck and head to another direction saying: "we woke up by the Lord of the morning. The boats have not yet crossed the sea (Nile)".

Farmers were coming back from the early boats. Pedestrians and riders were cursing sumpters and kidding with passers by. Dalliances, shouting, and laughter filled Al-Kumur's sky.

"Hurry, let us catch up the group descending into the valley."

"We are going back. Where are you going?"

The two groups met accidentally at the edge of the valley.

"The wind, driver of the sea, turned you back".

"It turned our boats back and broke our oars."

"Hey man – both you descenders (going down to the Nile) and ascenders (going up from the Nile) - is my son Bakheet with you?"

"We, descenders and ascenders, we have neither Bakkeet nor Saeed."

"Run and look for your son. The sea (Nile) is brimful and waves are sweeping."

She turned and jogged towards the River Nile.

Chapter (6)
Tales from Neighboring Villages

A chain of villages forming a circle around Al-Kumur starting from Nasri Island, Fangol, Wedi Al-Qubah, Al-Azozab, Al-Ja'liyeen, Al-Jabrab, Al-Hawaweer, Al-Galah, Al-Tarjamiyah, Um Zor, and Awlad (sons of) Wad Al-Fadul. The centerpiece of the necklace is a pearl overwhelmed by the glare of the sun and glittering of the Desert.

Every morning and before sunrise, inhabitants of neighboring villages hurry on their sumpters (donkeys and camels), pick-up trucks, and pedestrians towards Souk (market) Al-Kumur, schools, and agricultural lands. On the way they engage in talks and joking from the first rider to the last one and plan to return in the evening with blessings, tales, and hopes of a promising future.

At Khalwat Al-Faki Al-Turki, they disperse. Each heads to his location: market, restaurants and cafes, or cultivation in Al-Karo and escarpments. Some of them take the mud balls – green and yellow – and build walls before the flood. Buildings grow higher and life proceeds and retreats with the recession of the Nile.

Every village has a history, social activities, tales, poems, and jokes that relate it to the Nile, Desert, or the Mountain. These villages have strong social fabric, interrelated, connected, and flavored by Nasri Island.

Nasri Island is surrounded by water from all directions. It is the crossing point for family relations between east and west. Boats daily cross to east and west of the Island, take and bring things. But only lately and after the introduction of the ferry, people missed the conversations of boatmen (Mahmoud Wad Maiyah and Al-Nuwairi) and morning jokes.

Nasri Island

Nasri Island is divided into a number of Sawaqis (waterwheels) with quarters in the middle. Al-Saqiyah (waterwheel) is a name of the agricultural land. Al-Saqiyah is usually named after the grandfather of the family that owns it e.g. Saqiyah of Al-Sinaidab, Al-Alyab, Al-Doshab, Al-Kardab, Al-Zaidab, Al-Asaseem, Awlad (sons of) Farah, and Awlad (sons of) Maiyah. At the head of the Island there is the Saqiyah of Hamad Wad (son) Jadallah and Omar Wad Bashir etc.

Island Inhabitations agreed and built a road that crosses the Island from west to east known as the Middle Road. There are other subsidiary roads that link the vast area of the Island.

Members of Al-Ja'liyeen tribe live east of the Island, Al-Shaygiyah in the west, and a few of Al-Hassaniyah in the center. (These directions mean sunrise and sunset and not east and west of the Nile.)

Nasri Island wakes early on the voices of farmers going along the Middle Road. Donkey hooves are heard trotting towards Al-Sawaqi (waterwheels) or boat and ferry anchorage. Women patting the native loaf, hurly-burly, Al-Mavareek (wooden sticks with arrow-shaped fronts used for beating food during cooking) coming out of the thatched houses, smell of the Sudanese fermented or unleavened Kisrah dough (made of sorghum flour and cooked in fine sheets) smelled by pedestrians, and smoke blowing in the area between the farms and under the feet of pedestrians.

Inhabitants of Nasri Island are fond of living in it. They know no other place, yet they are proud of it. They cultivate, harvest, hold horse races in occasions, celebrate in evenings, and stay awake in nights chatting. They live on dates from palm trees, wheat, white sorghum, beans, corn, and milk. Their island suffices them of fruits and other crops.

Fangol Village

At the tip of Nasri Island, west of the Nile, there is the range of Fangol colored mountains where the British army camped and concluded its preparations for the Battle of Karari and access of Omdurman.

The summit of the mountains overlooks the west and east of the Nile. You can see the houses flat and small in size, Omdurman minarets within the range of sight, and the Nile underneath.

On a low land between the mountains appear Fangol houses linked with the lines of valleys as a contour drawing.

The British army chose the summit of Fangol mountains for camping before accessing Omdurman for the leader of the army thought that the armies of Al-Mahadiyah, led by Al-Khalifah (Caliph) Abdullah Al-Ta'ishi, would attack them in that region. So the British barricaded themselves with a stone wall known as Hosh Al-Kafir (Courtyard of the Unbeliever). The ruins of this wall are still there.

Antiques, which invading soldiers took from Al-Barkal, Karimah, and Kaboshiyah, were buried in this region. Over the time, grandsons of the British army arrived in the region carrying maps and looking for the buried antiques. Some of them were lucky to find the buried antiques. Some of these antiques are still buried there.

Al-Hassaniyah tribe lives in Fangol. Fangol Mountains contain a variety of the colored limestone, which girls use for painting houses in Eids (feasts – Lesser and Greater Bairams). In the near future paint companies will be happy with Fangol Lime Mountains.

If Fangol village could be transferred to the top of the mountains, the low land of the village could be transformed into a lake for storing drinking and irrigation Nile water.

Fangol Mountains are meters away from the River Nile. If the Nile and Mountains unite the green color will decorate the top of the mountains, vast land will change into a spring, and desertification and drought will be stopped.

Al-Biraiyab

Al-Biraiyab is not a village. It is a group of domes in a thick forest with a lot of movements around it. Islamic scholars were buried under these domes, which changed into shrines and graves where visitors, shepherds, and some dervishes roam this forest.

These domes were anciently built between Fangol and Wedi (small vlley) Al-Qubah (dome). They were built for the three sons of Bari: Dafallah, Ali, and Bazbar. They were religious sheikhs and scholars. It is said that they came from Rubatab region and settled in this valley, opened Al-Khalawi (native religious schools) to memorize Holy Quran and learn Arabic. They taught people religious matters and as a result the region is named after them. That was before the British invasion.

Al-Biraiyab became famous and has followers and disciples who gathered around them for different purposes. The British took notice of the gathering around these religious Sheikhs and imposed heavy unbearable taxes on them. The people left their homes, Al-Khalawi, region, and dispersed in different parts of Sudan.

Some of the people lived in Omdurman and Al-Jazera in Wad Madani regions. Some of them left to western Sudan. Only Faki (religious teacher) Mahmoud Abu Shara, his son Abdulrahman, and some Biraiyab families stayed in the region.

Seyad Bari, former President of Somalia, is from the Biraiyab family. Some natives of the region used to frequent visits to Seyad Bari.

Origins of many rulers of neighboring countries are traced back into the Sudan e.g. the mother of sister Egypt's President Mohammed Najeeb is from Wad Madani region, the mother of President Anwar Al-Sadat of Egypt is also from Omdurman, President Eidi Amin of Uganda is from the tribes of Southern Sudan, and President Idris Dibe of Chad is from Darfur.

Al-Kumur region has absorbed the religious spirit that goes back to Biraiyab and Sufi education. It taught people how to face life with the least and death with eyes of faith. They took from it the wisdom of asceticism and austerity that shrouds the Sufi life in Sudan. They receive the new born baby with voicing the calling to prayer in his ears and farewell their dead chanting:

"I conclude my utterance with prayers upon Prophet (PBUH). Oh Allah may You always pray upon and bless Prophet Mohammed, his companions, and forefathers. A prayer that excels musk in glorified fragrance."

They pour down soil on the grave of the deceased and go for their cultivation and picking.

These domes still have reverence in the souls of natives of the region. This awe is stemming from the respect of people to anyone who adheres to beliefs of Islam. The domes became a cemetery with religious tales and surrounded by a thick forest of

Laloub, mimosa, and acacia trees called the forest of Awlad (sons of) Bari.

Wedi Al-Qubah

It was called the small creek. But now it is Wedi (small wadi) Al-Qubah (dome). It separates the forest of Awlad (sons of) Bari from Al-Azozab. This small valley wrestles every year with its seasonal floods. It is one of the Sahara Desert tributaries and its sands are rich with Arabism and Arabic poetry.

Men and women of the valley compose poetry in their daily conversations and deliberations. Wad (son of) Nafie and his son Qurashi, and Abu Diraiqah are examples.

Abu Diraiqah says: "Oh, Allah I am tested by every thing from you. My eyes neither see thee nor do I reach your limits. Oh, you who hear the secrets and who has a wide extension. I am harmed by the girl that shrouded in the beauty you have granted her."

He said these verses after he repented and abandoned the old Arab custom of Al-Hambatah (taking one's camels forcibly and distribute them among the poor.)

Al-Hambata (plural of Hambati) - those who practice Al-Hambatah - do not steal, but take camels forcibly. They sell and distribute the camels among the needy. Al-Hambati (singular of Hambata) takes few camels for entertainment and spends them with his boy/girl friends.

Al-Hambatah is one of the practices of some poor, brave, and generous inhabitants of Arabia Peninsula called "Sa'leeq" e.g. Ta'batah Sharan, Al-Silaik bin Al-Salkah, Al-Shanfarah etc. they love chivalry and poetry.

Al-Hambatah poetry depicts their courage and describes their camels, lovers, and difficulties they have encountered and how they overcame them. The most famous of them in Sudan is Al-Tayyeb Wad Dhahawiyah from Jabal Um Ali village, north of Kaboshiyah, and his friend Taha

Al-Dhareer from the Arabs of Al-Butanah plains.

Al-Azozab Village
This village is built on top of a pebbly plateau that extends from the north and narrows in the south as a spearhead that is about to strike the Nile. It is one of the Desert's armies.

Inhabitants of Al-Azozab village are from Al-Hassaniyah Arabs: Awlad (sons of) Abdulaziz. A member of this village died and we went to burry him in the cemetery of Awlad (sons of) Bari. I was amazed of the number of attendants. I turned to Faraj Wad Al-Huwar and asked him astonishingly:

"Does Al-Hassaniyah tribe have this big number?"

Faraj: "Hey man, the Desert behind Al-Kumur is abounding with Al-Hassaniyah."

He added: "Hey man, Al-Hasaniyah has neither education nor traveling. They stay close to women and keep breeding!"

After the funeral ceremony was over by reading Al-Ratib (a religious book compiled by Imam Al-Mahdi) and beseeching Allah to be merciful upon the deceased, the gathering dispersed.

Three young boys from Al-Hassaniyah rode on a donkey. One of them fell because he wanted to ride with his back opposite to his brother's back. The donkey moved and he fell on the ground. He quickly stood up and changed his position. Farah laughed and said: "Aha look!" I remembered the story of Al-Hassaniyah famous donkey race!! (It was said that Imam Al-Mahadi sent a messenger to Al-Hassaniyah tribe to join him in jihad. They replied that they would join him after the end of the donkey race! Imam Al-Mahadi said "look! What are the people doing and what Al-Hassaniyah is doing?!!)

Members of Al-Hassaniyah tribe do not like immigration or even traveling to Khartoum, for fear of leaving their folks, doubt of not coming back, and love to roaming Al-Kumur market. They do not go farther than the market except for cultivation in Wad Hamid basin. They spend the whole day inside the market and go back to their homes with blessings of that day where they breed goats and sheep.

A handsome youth called Sulaiman appeared among Al-Hassaniyah tribe. He was famous for his smartness and elegance. Al-Hassaniyah girls composed love poetry about him. One of them said:

"He is sitting in *Malamah* (a gathering) and reading about *Mouhimah* (something important). Oh mother, Sulaiman is the sugar of *Al-Matamah* (city)."

Another girl responded by saying:

"Oh that polished gold. I was told he stood up and descended. Oh mother, May I be a tanned skin for Sulaiman to perform his prays on!"

Of course by saying "polished gold" she is referring to the fair skin of the beloved Sulaiman as Al-Hassaniyah is a fair colored tribe. By descended she meant he went down to the farms near the Nile. And by a tanned skin she wished she could be so close to him like the tanned skin for Sulaiman to perform his prays on.

A third girl also responded by saying:

"I wish I was at his age so I can breach limits of religion. Oh mother, Sulaiman's chest is like the door of a Christian (i.e. made by a Christian)."

These poems spread among Al-Hassaniyah and descended to Souk Al-Kumur and neighboring villages.

One day, one of my pals was sitting beside his father in Souk Al-Kumur among a group of merchants. There came a man walking towards them with other four men. Eyes of merchants were attracted to the advancing group and focused on one of them. The man walking in the middle was attractive as a magnet. One of the merchants said:

"Look at that man, doesn't he feel ashamed! He darkens the edges of his eyelids with kohl and goes into the market!"

Another merchant replied: "what do you mean?"

The third merchant said: "Hey man, this man does not darken his eyelids with kohl. His eyes are natural!!"

The four men came in the direction of the group of merchants, whose eyes were attracted to them, and exited from the north gate of the market. It was a phantom of beauty that shrouded the group of merchants all of a sudden and pleased them.

Things changed in merchants' eyes and ecstasy of magical beauty spread in them and a moment of clearness and generosity covered their souls. The merchants ordered breakfast and competed to pay the price. It was an unfamiliar gesture; for they eat together but each has to pay his share as in the famous Sudanese proverb "eat as brothers but pay as merchants."

Al-Ja'liyeen Village

There is no separating natural space between Al-Azozab and Al-Ja'liyeen villages except for the social difference in the nature of the human being in belonging to his group. We also find it in features of figures and natures. But it totally disappears in big occasions.

Al-Ja'liyeen tribe in this region does not migrate, for they live extravagant material life. They inherited money and vast agricultural lands, from their forefather, on both banks of the Great Nile. One can speak without reservation about their living in Al-Karo,. The "Sheikhdom of the Line (of villages)" winded up with them in an ancient era and they preceded others in the political awareness.

Al-Ja'liyeen agricultural lands found in Nasri Island, Al-Karo, Um Bagarah, on the two banks of the Nile, and behind Fangol Mountains at the borders of Al-Jiraif, Salwah, and Bawaleed justify that they are the "Arabs of the Banks".

Immigration has many features, but sometimes compulsory. It is said that Sheikh Ali Jadallah – Sheikh of the Region's Line – in one of his tours inside Nasri Island, was riding a bridled white donkey and passing through the Middle Road, stopped for some reason or other beside a farm of one of his cousins. Following a hot discussion between Sheikh Ali Jadallah and his cousin the Sheikh slapped his cousin in the face. His cousin did not retaliate, put down his pickax and went out of the Island and never came back.

He went to Um Dam region in western Sudan, got married and blessed with many children and made an extended family. He called his daughters and sons after his cousins in the region of Nasri Island. He named his sons Ali, Jadallah, Mohammed Khair, Abdulhafeez, Abdulwahab, and Bashir. He established Al-Jadallab tribe in western Sudan.

Souls are still attracted to the place of the original family and kinsfolk. Bodies disintegrated in the graves, but the seeds carried on forever.

Mohammed bin Khair Ali Jadallah traveled to western Sudan and married one of the granddaughters of the family in Um Dam.

Fatuity and tolerance are a contrast in the nature of Al-Ja'liyeen. They have also inherited virtuousness and generosity from the Arabs. They were the last people who migrated from Nasri Island and built their new houses west of the Nile parallel to the ruins of their old houses inside Nasri Island.

Individuals of Al-Ja'liyeen tribe access their farms in Nasri Island in the morning as if they are visiting a beloved character that they missed for quite a long time. If boats happen to anchor beside their old houses they jump from them as fishes that come up and plunge once again in the Nile. They say: "Salute, Nasri."

Al-Ja'liyeen stand with their high figures on the land of the Island every early morning at sunrise and say: " May Allah bless us with this sunrise." They remember the pump of

Hamad Wad Al-Omdah (Hamad son of the mayor) and the good days of the engineer and driver Wad Al-Sa'eed (son of the south), friend of the poet and inspector Abdulmajed Wad Al-Hasan who said:

"Among the drivers Wad Al-Sa'eed is well known. He touched the cam and ignited the ammunition."

At that time Hamad's pump was irrigating Nasri Island from the nearest to the farthest places – from Um Rahao (a place abounding with flocks of cranes) to the eastern region; and from Um Dalaleek (plural of Dalookah, a Sudanese female drum) up to the tip of the Island.

When pupils of Al-Kumur's elementary school are unable to solve mathematical questions, teacher Mahjoob Al-Sa'em loses his temper and piles soil onto them from the door and windows of the classroom. The pupils usually take care and keep an eye on him. When he loses his temper they say:" Aha, Hamad's pump has started."

Al-Jabrab Village

They trace back their ancestry to Jaber. They are the owners of Al-Khalawi for teaching Arabic language and memorization Holy Quran; and also have their own supplications and praises in their night meetings and solitude.

Some natives of Al-Kumur see in the political movement of Al-Jabrab a new gesture that does not go with their quietude and piety and may cause them to lose part of their religious reverence and respect. They disagreed with Al-Kumur, the old ally, in a political stance. As a result Al-Kumur natives mocked at them and called them the Vatican. This name now refers to their village.

The Vatican (Al-Jabrab Village) is a religious community that fears every new thing. When a sign was erected to show the direction of Al-Ja'liyeen Village, they discussed the matter with Al-Faki (scholar) Omar Bashir, a member of Al-Ja'liyeen tribe. They also later protested against settling Al-Hawaweer tribe beside them.

I am speaking about Al-Jabrab of the middle. But Al-Jabrab natives behind Al-Kumur live between Al-Thorah Kabotah and Hajar Al-Tair (mount of birds). The front Jabrab lives in Salwah region and they are called Awlad (sons of) Jaber.

Wad Al-Twaim is one of Awlad Jabir. Dr. Wad Badi, the poet, said about him:

"Breezes of Dighaish (early morning) diffuse pleasant odor and spill soul in the selves.

The wounded by waterwheels is lamenting and beseeching support from Sheikh Wad Al-Twaim. I am the wounded, I am wounded."

The Sheikh used to say his usual section or part of the Holy Quran that glorifies Allah Almighty: "Glory to Allah, the Most Holy; Glory to Allah, the Most Holy." Wad Al-Twaim was also famous for treating jaundice with Quranic verses and a touch of a hand.

In Al-Jabrab Village there is the Khalwah of Sheikh Mukhtar Wad Abdulraheem, who was a struggler (mojahid). Due to a defect in his legs, he used to crawl on his hands to teach Arabic language and Holy Quran. Musa and Bashir, of the generation of the 60's, are some of his students. His Khalwah was famous for Faza'h (resorting to it for security or help), Wednesday's Karamah (generosity, usually boiled durra or millet spiced with salt), and Sharafah (when a pupil ends a part of the Holy Quran, he takes his board with some verses of the Holy Quran on it and tours the village for alms.)

Awlad (sons of) Al-Jabrab are interested in education and sports. They form one football team with Al-Kumur. When students come in holidays in big numbers, they form a team especially for them and play matches against Al-Kumur. The Vatican (Al-Jabrab Village) cheers and encourages.

Al-Hawaweer Village

Al-Hawaweer landed as a one winged bird on the black castle between Al-Jabrab and Galat (castle) Al-Bakriyah where they built their houses. They are traced back to the Arabs of North Africa that roam the desert. Al-Huwari (singular of Hawaweer) is a name heard a lot in Algeria and Libya.

Al-Hawaweer left Kaboshiyah region and Jabal Um Ali, east of the River Nile, and headed northwards to Al-Shaygiyah dwellings after a conflict with Al-Tayyb Wad Dhahawiyah. Some of them later came back to west of the Nile to form their village between Al-Jabrab and Galat Al-Bakriyah.

They still practice the green tattoos on women's cheeks. It is one of the practices of the Bedouins in the Great Sahara. They are not Nilotics, but natives of the oases.

Galat (Castle of) Al-Bakriyah

The castle is a name of the 8th arch around Al-Kumur inhabited by many families. They do not stand up with Al-Shaygiyah with all their strength, and neither support Al-Ja'liyeen nor Al-Jabrab.

One of the peddlers, from a Nigerian origin, came to the region some time ago looking for livelihood, when the Sudanese pound was in its full strength. He got married to one of Galah (castle) girls and was blessed with very beautiful and decent girls.

Due to some difference in Souk Al-Kumur, the groups coming from Castle are called Falaleet (Nigerians) jokingly and sarcastically. Thus Falaleet became the name for their village for a long time. The village is traced back to their ancestor who descended from the Fulani tribes in West Africa and called Falatah (Nigerians) in Sudan.

After a long time the Castle inhabitants became fed up with this name and their dissatisfaction was clear. As a result it was called the Castle once more, because it was far away from the Nile lands and Al-Karo. Some people add Al-Bakriyah to become Galat Al-Bakriyah.

When agricultural lands were distributed in Al-Karo, the share of Galat Al-Bakriyah natives was the sandy land lower Souk Al-Kumur. Haj Ahmed, the Falati (Nigerian), protested and said to Galat Al-Bakriyah Group: "they have given you a red land that resemble Dahiyat Al-Girid (the posterior of the ape)." As a result Dahiyat Al-Girid became the name of their agricultural lands.

On Dahiyat Al-Girid, round rooms called Al-Hiran were built where the wind, sand, and alluvium vapors revolve around them. When the Nile flood retreats the lands were cultivated with Hinaiteer, which its leaves are sold in the market and seeds stored with the rest of crops.

Families that inhabited the Castle were Hamid Haj Ahmed and Awlad (sons of) Rikaizi who were famous of treating blindness or white cataract know as (Al-

Shaloqah). They perfected and monopolized this profession and never relinquished it for anyone else. Delegations used to visit them from remote areas asking for treatment. My father tempted them with a lot of money to learn this profession but they refused.

Members of Awlad Maman, who are traced back to their ancestor Maman who lived in an area in northern Abyssinia, also inhabited the Castle. Linguistically, Maman in the Abyssinian language means believing or trusting. They have some branches in areas neighboring western Abyssinia in Kasala, Damazin, and Rusairis. Relations of neighborhood led to mutual migrations between northern Sudan and Axsom Kingdom in northern Abyssinia.

Behind Galat Al-Bakriyah at the eastern horizon mountains loom covered with pebbles and rugged valleys that flow into the sharp slope of Abu Hawiyah Valley. Sands draw overlapping and color contour lines on top of the mountains. Factors of erosion dropped from the walls materials of the viscous soil, which turned into solid heaps as mountains inside the rooms.

The dispersed houses of the Castle look as if they rolled off the eastern heights and suddenly stopped. They are located between the mountains and the turn of the valley. Some rooms are inserted into the edge of Abu Hawiyah Valley, so their edges are slanted. They shorten towards the valley and lengthen towards the mountains.

Between the Valley and Mountain, Axsom civilization met with the civilization of West Africa on the land of Nuba, linked by the Arabic language. Of this mixture appeared talents of the Castle's youths on theatre and football fields.

Al-Tarjamiyah Village

It is the 9th unit of the necklace around Al-Kumur. It is built on a flat sandy plain with mimosa and acacia trees, pasture of animals. The pastureland is not far away from the houses. Members of Al-Tarajmah tribe are pure Arabs in the language and nature. They visit Souk (market) Al-Kumur in groups called Al-Tarjamiyah Group.

Al-Tarjamiyah Group has a presence in Souk Al-Kumur. They are not merchants, but work with all and in all fields. They are characterized with a friendly nature and special intimate friendship. Hasabalrasool is the first owner of a complex composed of a Bakery, restaurant, and coffee shop.

When Al-Tarjamiyah Group enters the market, it stirs a clatter and chatter in the four corners. Ahmed Abu Safah (Abu Safah means he who puts a small ball of snuff between the teeth and lower lip), Taiallah, Hamdeen, and Fadulalmola, and Abudlwahid cause hurly-burly when they arrive and coffee shops and stores flourish and prosper.

The five men enter from one gate with their hands up. They curse this man, point to another, and prepare for wrestling with sharp tongues and hands. They have no animosities and love joking.

These five men are contented and do not rush for livelihood fearfully. They never worry, satisfy with the least, and never complain of misfortune. They go home with whatever they find and satisfy with what Allah has granted them. They leave Al-Kumur with a drink of water from the large jars of Al-Faki Al-Turky called Al-Darib (the road).

Um Zor Village

Um Zor (big chest) is surrounded by tales, secrets, and poems. Um Wardah (rose), one of Um Zor girls, married long time ago and her husband gifted a she-camel called Um Zor as a postponed dowry.

For some reason or another, the couple disagreed and divorced. The woman demanded her postponed dowry and the man procrastinated. They went to the Sheikh (chief) of the tribe to solve the problem. The man did not mention the dowry and claimed that Um Zor is that Castle behind Al-Kumur extended from northeast to southwest, and not a big breast she-camel. The Sheikh awarded her Jabal (mountain) Shamikh on a pebble land. Since that time the region is called Um Zor.

Um Zor Village is composed of mud-built rooms painted with animals' dung. The rooms have no courtyards in front of each of them, straw and wood-built houses beside them, or a Rakobah (a rectangular-shaped building with four or more wooden pillars thatched with grass as a verandah in front of a room used for cooking and midday nap) thatched with Tibes grass and Dahseer.

Names of Um Zor inhabitants came from the Desert e.g. Al-Ajami, Daba' (she-wolf), Wad Bilais, Wad Al-Sa'eyd, Omar Wad Nurallah, Al-Shiait Wad Montaha, and Um Wardah (rose). Women and men compose Arabic poetry. One of them is Omar Qirainat who said:

"It bruised the wood and talked to solid stones.

You are neither a pure Juhaini (Arab tribe) nor one who sits with Al-Hum.

I told you a speech that nauseates the soul.

But nostrils are plugged up and do not smell."

Um Zor is the nearest village to Souk (market) Al-Kumur, at the entrance of the Animals Souk (Market), between Migaiteeah and Qala' Wad Al-Fadul at the house of Al-Hajah bint Zainaldeen. Um Zor natives participate in the market activities. They enter the market with their commodities of traditional Arabic poetry and animals.

Souk Al-Kumur was once used to gather poets such as Omar Qirainat, Wad (son of) Ashmaiq, Abdulmajid Wad Al-Hasan (the inspector), Wad Ibrahim, and Salih Wad Owaidhah.

Omar Qirainat, the poet, stretched his limbs at the door after been beaten in the whist and said:

"Tonight Al-Kumur launched its *Hawon* (mortar guns).

That; made me take the lead and put my cards down."

The group of five – Al-Tarjamiyah Group – met and said: "we knew all that talk. But what is "down"?

Hamdeen: "Now, isn't it an English word?"

Let us go to Wad Mahmoud, who was then in the intermediate school, sitting with his father in the shop. Ahmed Abu Safah was leading the group.

Ahmed Abu Safah: "Omar, what does (down) mean?"

Omar: "Down means descend to the lower."
Ahmed Abu Safah turned to the group and said:

"Look at your pal Qirainat. He speaks English!"

They jogged inside the market, went around pillars, verandahs, and inside stores, shops, and mills. They entered from the front door of the restaurant and exited from the back door looking for the poet Wad Ashmaiq, the eldest poet. When they came down from the flourmill of Sheikh of the Line (of villages), Ali Wad Siddiq met them and said:

"Hey men, I have put my share of money, what is the matter with you?"

Ahmed Abu Safah: "Hey man, you haven't seen what Wad Ashmaiq has done!"

Ali Wad Siddiq: "Here beside you in Al-Nur's coffee shop."

They lined up in the middle of the coffee shop and found him sitting in the verandah at the entrance. Wad Ashmaiq stopped the cup of tea near his mouth and looked at them and said:

"What is wrong with you folks?"

Taialla: "look at your friend, sitting and drinking tea!"

Hamdeen: "he is also crossed-legged and drinking tea!"

Ahmed Abu Safah: "What a temperament?"

Wad Ashmaiq: "Hey men, what is the matter with you?"

Ahmed Abu Safah extending his hands near Wad Ashmaiq's face: "Where are you sitting? And where have you been? Qirainat started to compose English poetry!"

Abdulwahid laughs and turns to Fadulalmola, takes the snuff box, rubs his hands and says: "Your snuff is good."

Wad Ashmaiq: "What Qirainat has said?"

Fadulalmola touches Ahmed Abu Safah: "Say the poem, please."

Ahmed Abu Safah chants the words of the poet Qirainat while Wad Ashmaiq watches the mocking eyes of the group:

"Tonight Al-Kumur launched its *Hawon* (mortar guns). That; made me take the lead and put my cards down."

Hamdeen addressing Wad Ashmaiq: "Aha, what does 'down' mean?"

Ahmed Abu Safah: "may Allah inflict you with a disease."

Taiallah: "By Allah, you era has elapsed poor Wad Ashmaiq!"

Abdulwahid: "By Allah, Qirainat has beaten you."

Wad Ashmaiq said go and tell him the following verses. He composed on the spot: "she is a girl of decent and powerful folk who never dispute in trifles. And by seduction of girls my bones lied down at *Kawon*."

Ahmed Abu Safa: "please, say it again so we can memorize it."

Hamdeen addressing the group" take care of this word "Kawon", do not miss it, and let us go to Wad Mahmoud."

Ali Wad Siddiq met them for the second time accompanied by Mohammed Wad Jubarah.

Ali Wad Siddiq laughing: "Hey folk, what is the result?"

Ahmed Abu Safah: "hey man step back. By Allah, those guys became truly crazy. By my faith, they have started to compose English poetry."

Ahmed Abu Safah talking to Wad Mahmoud: "Listen man, come here please."

Hamdeen added: "we want you to explain the meaning of the last word."

Wad Mahmoud: "Kawon, Kawon. I am not sure but there is "coins" and it means changes." Taiallah shouted and jumped in the air:" hey folk, he means that the girl left his bones as coins."

Taiallah turns to the group: "Hey folks, I swear by the Prophet, these poets are crazy. They say poetry in English!"

Fadulalmola who talked least: "Qirainat and Wad Ashmaiq! Where did they learnd English?!"

Ahmed Abu Safah: "This is the Satan of poetry."

The shadows in the market extended eastwards and the noise of hitting the doors and thrust of locks were frequently heard.

Haj Mohammed and his sons got ready to return to Salwah Village. Bint (daughter of) Bashir shouted in front of the coffee shop: "the livelihood has flown away. Livelihood has vanished."

Everyone packed the rest of his commodities. The commodities of Um Zor and Tarjamiyah are remains of speech from the old Arabic poetry.

Ahmed Omar Nurallah is now a strong and cheerful youth since adolescence. He tours Souk Al-Kumur as if looking for something. He is fond of journeys with the car of Wad Fatootah and Al-Tahir.

Ahmed has a very close relationship with the drivers and their helpers. He drives from Souk Al-Kumur and gets down opposite to Um Zor. He abstained from working in his family's agricultural lands at the tip of Al-Turky's noria. His destination was different, neither the Nile nor the Desert. He desires the confluence of the two (White and Black) Niles. He aspires to the life of the Capital.

Ahmed went to Omdurman and started to port boxes, broker, and trade. Finally he owned a store in the vegetable and fruit market in Omdurman and hired a house near the market.

Ahmed's rented house was a destination for Um Zor natives. They lodged in it not as guest but as owners. He used to receive and be generous to them, prepare them for the journey back home, give them money, especially the needy, and see them off with wishes of meeting again – if not with the same people it will be with others. His house was a terminal for his folks.

He died before he could marry and left behind a good memory. Um Zor and the neighboring villages missed him very much. Men and women mourned him, Al-Nihas (a big copper drum) was beaten, mourning songs were melodized and tribal chiefs and youths escorted him to his final resting place.

People came from the defiles of Wedi Al-Qubah and Al-Azozab to mourn him. Riders from Al-Ja'liyeen, Al-Zaidab, Al-Doshab, and Al-Kardab came from Al-Kumur, Tarjamiyah, Abu Hawiyah valleys, Jabrab, and Bakriyah hastened to pay him the last honors. Al-Kumur sneaked for consolation from the western market gate, at the Animals Market between the bakery and flour mill.

Merchants shut their shops and trotted on Gala' Wad Al-Fadul for this great loss. Women hastened from all parts and the groups met behind the house of Wad Al-Bida'.

Delegations arrived and gatherings rushed from Jibal Al-Sadah (mountains of the masters). Awlad (sons of) Wad Abu Kawareek was shouting to each other on the backs of camels. Al-Zainab came from Al-Jabalab well, and Awlad Shuwain and Awlad Jufoon from Jabal Al-Atron. The delegations rolled down from Khor (gorge of) Al-Dalaib and Wadi Al-Mahraib to give their solace to the family of the deceased Ahmed Wad Omar Wad Nurallah.

The poet Qirainat bewailed him saying:
"The frowning and deceptive present life is the home of disappearance, undoubtedly.
It has a short shackle that you neither walk nor jog.
If the bad person dies, then he is gone and demolished
If the good dies, people mourn him a lot
Um Zor darkened, and look people are still weeping
The heavy hair is laid on the ground
The tribes are missing you from here to Makkah
Your soul is eternal and birds of heaven have perched on it."
This is an elegy for a star that shined in the sky of Um Zor and suddenly disappeared.
"Hurry up the procession of the funeral has moved. The elders are carrying hoes, spades, and pickaxes – with one or two opposite heads. They are going towards the forest of Awlad Bari."
They descended with the corpse towards Souk Al-Kumur and entered the market in

sad silence interrupted by the sound of footfall on the pebbles. Ahmed bid the market square and world of money and business the last farewell. The people exited from the lower gate at the old Harazah tree, towards the football field. His life was a short one. The crowd left the market and football field and crossed the valley of life to the cemetery.

On the separating screen between Al-Karo and sands, at the old Harazah tree, two birds croaked on remote branches. The Desert bird flew up in the air and the Nile bird snatched a book the wind was flipping on the roof of the court.

White she-camels led the procession of the funeral. The riders' legs looked like white wings on these camels. And at the back of the procession, there were horses with their saddles turned to the back.

Ahmed was a unique type of youths. He was from Awlad Nurallah who had other branches in Kumur, Shabasha, Karkooj, and Karm Al-Nuzol.

Human beings and animals scrambled to carry the coffin. As a result there was a great hurly-burly. (Women gathered in circles and walked with anklets, horses and donkeys were shackled, and camels growled in mourning.) Um Zor was not the only mourner, but even the palm trees and valleys. And the crows at Um Zor Castle croaked signaling the departure and separation of Um Ridah and the postponed dowry.

Good memories about the deceased were revived in the minds of mourners especially in Um Zor and Al-Kumur during the night of faithfulness.

He was a young man who was promising himself with the realization of old fanciful memories. He walked his short youthful journeys in broad day-light and moon-lit nights where sands of valleys were like islands on shallow water surfaces. Shadows of walls of abandoned courtyards were in awful serenity under the moon light. Ears of the night were listening to whispers, murmur of talks, and distant light heralding the fleeing of night.

Awlad Wad Al-Fadul Village
This village is composed of Awlad (sons of) Wad (son of) Al-Fadul and Awlad Wad Ahmed. Their houses are bordering the forest of their grandfather Ahmed and Khor (gorge) of Wad Al-Fadul. The village usually flourishes after the flood. But when they harvest they disperse and recede with the Nile's ebb.

One year, the Nile attacked and Al-Karo was inundated. But after the ebb, Awlad Wad Ahmed disappeared and left no trace. Where had they gone? No one knows. Only Othman and two sons of Mahjoob were left.

Awlad Wad Al-Fadul, Ali Wad Al-Haj, Balah, and Bilal built their houses beside the Khor (gorge) of their father directly linked to the Nile. They practiced various professions in addition to farming such as animal husbandry, trade in the Animals Market, and butchery. The dwellings of Wad

Al-Fadul changed into a village that combined between professions of the Nile and Desert.

From their homelands, four vehicle roads ramify: a desert road to Um Zor, a social road to the center of Al-Kumur, a commercial one to the heart of the Souk (market), and a Nile road to the football field.

Chapter (7)
Composition of Al-Kumur's Population: Original and Immigrant Names

Three tribes mixed in Al-Kumur. They were Al-Shaygiyah, Al-Ja'liyeen, and Al-Hassaniyah who united by Islam, language, neighborhood, and intermarriage which produced a generation of Al-Alyab, Al-Doshab, Al-Kardab, Al-Zaidab, Al-Sinaidab, Al-Ardab, Al-Kromab, Al-Hiraimab, Al-Sanaqiah, Al-Assaseem, Al-Fraseen, Al-Shabalil, etc.

Original Names

Names originating from the Nile are: Kababiya, Kindi, Qaoor, Kadaq, Doshi, Al-Dalti, and A'soom. Words originating from the Nile are: Yikadiq (hoeing small grass), Yikadin (hoeing grass from the canal), Yiteelan (irrigate plants for the second time), Al-Aroti (a part of the waterwheel where water pours into), and Al-Ashmaiq (a rope made of palm tree barks). The meanings of these words directly relate to eras in history and heritage of the old Nile in northern Sudan.

Immigrant Names

These names immigrated to Sudan from the east. They carry the influence of religion and desert e.g. Al-Sunni, Al-Waseelah, Al-Huwar, Mohammed, Ahmed, and names of prophets and orthodox caliphs. When the family grows it is called Bait (house) of so and so e.g. Awlad (sons of) Abdulqadir, Awlad Al-Sa'im, Awlad Myyah, Awlad Farah, Awlad Sha'r Al-Bal etc.

The impact of Islam and nature is clear in the names of women e.g. Fatimah, Jeddah, Makkah, Madinah etc.

Names that relate to the Nile are: Al-Shitail (transplant), Nakheel (palm trees), Al-Saraf (spring), Al-Neel (Nile).

Names that relate to the Desert are: Al-Hawad and Al-Hana. Names that relate to seasons are: Al-Shati (winter), Al-Hatif, Al-Haid, Al-Einah (torrential rains) etc. Some precious names such as: Al-Tibrah (gold nuggets), Nabtah (plant), Nafisah (precious), etc. there are also contemporary names that included the transparency of the poetical and musical words such as Abeer (fragrance), Nahid (bosomy), Anaheed (sighs), etc.

Names have histories and tales reflecting the echo of the past years and memories. They go from forefathers to grandsons and from generation to another since the era of Ba'nkhi, Nafertiti, and Kandakah (names of pharos) where they were found written on cowries and rocks inside tombs and cemetery buildings.

Quiet and Violent Movement of Population

Days expanded conceiving in their womb neighboring and coherent tribes in the lodging and treatment. By time and settlement, tribes quietly merged through marriages.

The quiet merging was followed by violence hidden by fate for the innocent inhabitants of the region. External and internal wars took them by surprise during eras of the

Turkish, British, and rule of Al-Khalifah (Caliph) Abdullah Al-Ta'ishi.

Ismael Pasha was killed in Shindi during the Turkish colonization which was followed by Al-Darfterdar Retaliatory Campaign. Al-Ja'liyeen and other tribes left their homelands. As a result Al-Kumur was a crossing point and settlement for some of them. Then after, Mahmoud Wad Ahmed group invaded Al-Matamah during the rule of Al-Khalifah (Caliph) Abdullah Al-Ta'ishi. The British followed after their victory in the Battle of Karari and the whole country was subjugated to the British Crown for quiet a long time, which granted inhabitants of the region stability that kept them away from wars and invasions.

Wars took inhabitants by surprise. Well-organized armies crossed the region, rocked it, and evoked compulsory immigration. Floods of inhabitants poured out of the region, while human waves and groups collided with each other between Al-Matamah and Al-Hugnah; and even farther.

Some tribes and families assembled around the region of Al-Kumur due to its central position between the 1st cataract and Shindi, west of the Nile. They entered Nasri Island as a hiding and peaceful abode.

Nasri Island gathered all crossing, hiding, and settling families with its natives. Ultimately the Island was overcrowded and the flood of 1946 drove some of these families out to Al-Kumur and neighboring villages.

The Nile flooded with water and alluvium. Grass grew up and greened. Trees grew leaves and bore fruits. Valleys poured down with blessings of the Desert. 'Arabs of the banks' cultivated the land and fished.

These were days of harvest - season of rejoicing - where youths got married. Some of them immigrated to his forefathers' regions such as Wad Baiya who headed northwards to his folks in Al-Shaygiyah homes, married Al-Na'oom, and came back with her to Al-Kumur.

Chapter (8)
Popular Tales and Proverbs
Departure of Al-Na'oom

Tales, stories, and games, are related to human being and nature of place with its beliefs and events of history that enrich arts, literature, and social life.

Once two persons meet in Al-Kumur, they begin to talk about popular proverbs and tales such as the tale of Al-Na'oom departure which has become a proverb.

It was said that Salim Wad Babiya had gone to his folks in the northern land, married Al-Na'oom, and departed with her to Al-Kumur as a second wife over the first one Sarorah bint babiya.

Al-Na'oom said: "the month of Rajab is the season of scything dates." She adds: "Allah willing, next year I will be with my folks in the north." She was blessed with three girls. The girls married and she was blessed with grandchildren and still yearning to go to her folks in the season of scything dates. More than forty years elapsed and she was hoping to accomplish that journey! Woe unto anyone who postpones his journey in Al-Kumur's community for one or two days! People will say the same about him. Some one will say: "your journey is typical to Al-Na'oom's."

Al-Na'oom was a leader who used to take reins of women's gatherings. If a man talks a lot in a gathering some one will interrupt him by saying: "how can I have a chance to speak while Al-Na'oom is present!"

Al-Na'oom's share of dates comes to her with its original names e.g. Al-Barakawi, Al-Jao, bit Tamodah, and Al-Qindail; and with its desert colors e.g. yellow and red pressed dates, Al-Karmoshah etc. Al-Na'oom sorts out dates and recalls immigrant names and says: "these are the dates of Um Al-Khair transplant, and this is the date palm of my (maternal) uncle Sayyed Ahmed."

Some people do not regard Al-Na'oom's speech as some sort of imagination or lying; especially after she proves it is true. She distributes dates among neighbors and says: "please, taste our dates. May Allah increase date palms and dates and we could afford to distribute. Say amen.

The Lie Committee

Al-Kumur abounds with popular and official committees for schools, courts, collection of donations, village representation etc. Under these committees there are committees that enrich social life such as the Lie Committee, and Committee of Wad Abu Sikeen group etc.

Members of the Lie Committee are: Al-Sunni, Wad Al-Huwar, Abdulwahab, Wad Myyah, Al-Maryoud, and Wad Bakhait. This committee has a code and regulations, sessions and meetings, judges, members, announcements, bailiffs, spies, oaths, fines, jails etc.

Al-Kumur's meetings abound with people in front of the small shops, especially Abbas Wad Al-Hidai's shop. If one speaks and exaggerates and the people doubt that he has evoked a subject of truth and fantasy or tends to lie, rumors circulate in Al-Kumur's community.

Evidences of cases are laughter, astonishment, sarcasm, and condemnation. If people laughed and others astonished, mocked or denounced, then the village community would request the Lie Committee to hold a meeting to follow up, investigate and incriminate.

The claimant who submitted the lawsuit would be announced. They deliberate and the true liar is known. They announce him and his family that the committee is going to drink the evening tea with him and that his wife, sons, daughters, and may be some neighbors have to attend especially if the lie was a big one. Oh, how terrible is frankness and presentation before one's own family!!

Speech is stired by investigation and accusation. The meeting is held, prosecution and defense start, and finally the conviction. There is a lawyer who defends the accused, another opposing lawyer who sets traps for him, and a neutral judge. The testimony of the family of the accused is not acceptable.

When the accused is convicted, he is mocked at in front of his family, fined, and has to perform a social work. So people avoid telling lies. As a result a community that appreciates truth, but not devoid of fantasies that are not far away of lies, is established.

Group of Wad Abu Sikeen

Abu Sikeen is a member of this group that inhabited the northeastern part of Al-Kumur. He married and was blessed with children. His daughters also married and left for Khartoum, Shindi, and east of the Nile. The boys also dispersed after marriage.

Abu Sikeen and his wife go for farming in Nasri Island. Men go alone to the boats and women lead another road to the boats. But Abu Sikeen and his wife never separate.

Abu Sikeen and his wife, contrary to the villagers, isolate themselves from men and women. They go together. He helps her get into Wad Myyah's boat, sit side by side, and sometimes he reserves for her beside him or otherwise. They keep talking on the boat; collaborate in the field, take meals and return home together, and exchange cigarettes. People speak a lot about them, but they don't care.

Wad Abu Sikeen meets his wife's requirements and he is proud that he obeys her. Thus he is against the mainstream of the village community. He publicly brags of doing so in front of those who denounce his actions.

So everyone who obeys his wife in Al-Kumur is regarded as one of Abu Sikeen's group. As a result men do not declare agreement in points of view with their wives for fear they might be classified as members of Wad Abu Sikeen's group. But Wad Abu Sikeen declares that in big congregations when people meet in happy and sad occasions.

The story of Abu Sikeen was conveyed to neighboring villages, Shandi, Al-Thorah, and Omdurman. People started, in every community, to classify the Group of Wad Abu Sikeen till he had a party with heads, members, and candidates.

Al-Tayyeb Wad Abdulmalik took Wad Abu Sikeen Group system to Kinanah and Othman Al-Hasan Abu Hijail took it to Wad Sulfab.

I was amazed while living in Riyadh, Kingdom of Saudi Arabia, of a discussion between the guest and one of the invitees in the house of my neighbor who was hosting his brother-in-law (husband of his wife's sister) during the dinner that the guest said: "hey men, I think this man is one of the Group of Wad Abu Sikeen!!" I couldn't talk of the surprise and stopped eating, not because of the name or the story, but for the way he talked. I thought he was one of Al-Kumur's natives. I was dead sure that he belonged to that place!!

After we finished eating and washed our hands, I said to him:

"Hey man, do you have relatives in Al-Kumur?"

He replied: "where is this Al-Kumur?

I said to him: "Al-Kumur, the only one, near Shandi."

He said to me: "No. by Allah, but we have another Kumur in Al-Jazerah, Wad Madani near Wad Sulfab."

Till this moment he did not know why the question is asked. Then he said to me: "Why?"

I said to him: "because of this tale of Wad Abu Sikeen."

He said: "by Allah, it is a famous tale in Wad Sulfab."

I was certain that Othman Abu Hujail was the one who took it to the community of Wad Sulfab. Al-Tayyeb Abdulmalik laid down a rule for it in Rabak City and Kosti region. It was not easy to be a member in the Group of Wad Abu Sikeen. He also made special law for the newly wedded couples. It was not enough to dig a smoke hole (smoke and steam sauna) for your wife, put some

Talh and sandal woods in it, and kindle fire. That was not enough!! But you ought to dig the hole with certain measurements and widen its circumference for bigger amount of incense woods. Al-Tayyeb cunningly says: "powerful fires and dense smoke makes tambourine tight and hot!!"

The other term is to buy Natie (the mat around the smoke hole for the naked woman to sit on) and carry it in broad daylight. But if you disguise and feel shy while carrying it, you do not deserve the membership of the Group of Wad Abu Sikeen. Al-Tayyeb says: "Al-Shamlah (a woolen cover wrapped around the body of a woman during the smoke sauna) is not necessary, because it is a task of the mother-in-law."

The last and important term is to henna the hands and feet of the woman. Of course the woman can not move or take something. The husband serves her and meets her demands. Only at that point, he deserves the membership of the Group of Wad Abu Sikeen.

If you would ever visit Al-Kumur, you have to endure tricks and jokes. The people here play with language and meanings that you would not be able to understand.

Ali Kish Kish

Ali Kish Kish is a youth from east of the Nile. He has family relations with folks in Nasir Island and Al-Kumur. He was a tall, intelligent, and handsome youth, with strong physique, harmonized muscles, graceful, and moves briskly.

People say Ali was playing differently in his childhood. He used to play with birds, lurk for them and catch them swiftly. He used to chase games and rabbits. When he grew up he used to run with dogs and catch their tails and race with horses.

Ali Kish Kish is always clean in his body and clothes. He puts on tiger-skin shoes, native shirt, and long trousers. He was fond of wearing his garment on the Sudanese style with the Swiss textile turban.

Ali Kish Kish never shook hands with anyone while sitting. He usually stands up hurriedly for greeting with his tall physique, extends his vivid strong hand with distinct blood vessels on the back of it and forearm. He stretches the words of greetings and says: "how... are... you... man." He attracts you till you look him in the eyes. At this moment you no doubt will trace him back to the ancestry of Naga' Kings in the ancient Nuba eras.

Ceremonies and occasions are not held until Ali Kish Kish attends. If he is late, young girls sing:

"Ali Kish Kish why did not he come? Vial of sprinkling fragrance, why not come?"

When he is seen coming from a distance, women ululate (utter trilling cries of joy) in the back row and girls increase the beating of Dalookah (a Sudanese female drum). Children chant and old and young people rejoice at his coming, wittiness, courtesy, and humor.

Ali sits with children, and elders laugh when he speaks frankly about the facts of their childhood and say: "yes Ali, by Allah you have said the truth. May Allah curse your Satan?"

Ali was one of the youth groups who attend parties in neighboring villages. Every village regards him as a member of it. If it is necessary, he crosses the Nile swimming in mid nights to attend a party in west of the Nile. He puts his clothes on top of his head and boasts that the water does not wet his back.

Ali Kish Kish perfected fencing and he could defend himself against three duelers from striking him simultaneously during fights that occur in these parties. He mocks at anyone who wants to whip him and provokes him with obscene words while putting down his clothes in the center of the circle in preparation for the whipping. He does this to overdo the challenge and manifest manhood.

Whipping is a custom from central Africa. Men used to whip women as a token of love then they marry them afterwards. This custom is changed so that men are whipped in front of women in celebrations of some tribes of northern Sudan.

Ali Kish Kish came to visit his relatives in Al-Kumur and Nasri Island. He spent some days with them and attended a happy occasion of Awlad Al-Huwar. As he was simple, good- hearted, and loved to help others he tucked up his trousers and started collecting grass with his peers to feed the animals.

But work is as speech, a way to fathom and know depths of selves. Ali suddenly was changed in the eyes of Nasri Island's girls and they twisted the song of the east Nile girls to say:

Ali Kish Kish, why didn't he come? He who scythed grass, why didn't he come?

I don't know the reason for this song! Was it because he was modest and scythed the grass or because he got married from one of the east Nile girls from Al-Basabeer and Galat (castle) Wad Jamal?

Al-Basabeer and Al-Kumur have a relation similar to that of the two Niles (white and blue). Saleh Wad Ewaidah, Al-Kumur's poet, said about Al-Basabeer:

"I want to complain to you as you are the elder. I want to complain to you as you are the expert. Goz (sand dune) Al-Basabeer did not satisfy me. It hammered me with seven nails. One in Al-Zareer (.....) hitting the short, another in the backbone that made Al-Tinaigeer (.....), and a third in rib that made me Agheer (.....)."

He mentioned seven locations in his exhausted body hammered by Al-Basabeer's nails. He ends his poem by saying:

"I have to be a crocodile and lurk in Al-Keer (....), in Al-Sidder (Christ's thorn) before Al-Basabeer. Feed in the blood, snatch, and carry."

Ali Kish Kish went to Al-Basabeer. As a result Al-Kumur's girls mocked at him and twisted the song. They also mocked Ahmed

Abu Safah when one girl sang with her peers in the wedding of her brother. All came out of the center of the circle (the place for singing and dancing). Ahmed Abu Safah spent a lot of time in dancing and showing his manhood. He was jumping in the air very seriously and the girls were singing, ridiculously saying:

"Oh amorous girl, Kisrah (thin sheets of maize dough cooked in a hot baking tin) is good with Tagliyah (dried shreds of meat, minced and cooked with onion, oil, and spices), Oh boy!"

The group of Al-Tarjamiyah: Hamdeen, Taiallah, and Fadulalmola were calling him with high voices to come out. But he was neither hearing nor seeing. He was jumping in the air, and with each jump he took one step forward and another backward in balance with the beatings of Al-Dalookah (a Sudanese female drum).

Taiallah jumped to Ahmed Abu Safah and caught him. Ahmed tried to escape him and to proceed. Taiallah hurried and said to him:

"The girls are laughing at you. Listen to what they say."

Ahmed paid attention, laughed, and raised his both hands to the girls and said: "Here it is. May Allah curse you?" All laughed and he exited the circle.

Al-Kumur's natives mock even themselves for entertainment and jokes. Wad Al-Asad looked at his face in the mirror, conjoined and tightened his lips, contracted his eyebrows, and swore: "By Allah the Greatest, I usually don't feel bored or frustrated till I look my face in the mirror."

Every thing in Al-Kumur stems from the Nile, even the jokes and mockeries which increase with the Nile's flood and decrease with its recession. In mid September each year the Nile usually sneaks back to its course after a long expansion on the lands. The days of leisure and jokes are now over and people begin work.

The Nile leaves behind interrupted lakes where the slim white cow birds gather around. Half the eyes of oysters which are submerged in the mud focus on Al-Kumur. The soil-colored flocks of sand grouse leave every early morning from its nests in the Desert towards the Nile flapping their wings above Al-Kumur. They land near the water; snatch oysters, feed on small creatures of these remote lakes carefully, and sound jubilantly on their way back to the Desert.

In the summer season the Nile current is quiet. Waves splash on the Nile's banks, water and souls are clean, jokes and mockeries abound in the fields.

Moist and dry crops are harvested, dates dry up, hay is sorted out, and beans are packed and stored. Sheep and goats mate, cows beget and Souk (market of) Al-Kumur abounds in commodities. Merchants exchange dry measures and balances. Animals are slaughtered and butchers shout at each other. Gristmills rumble, flour is ground, and dough is ready. Bags of milk are moved. Al-Kumur's children play football on Dahiyat Al-Qird (posterior of the ape).

Trucks are packed with crops to be sold in Souk (market of) Omdurman. Families renew their clothes and furniture. Scarves are sewed for grooms and marriages are contracted in the mosque and Khalwat Al-Turki. Nights abound in joys and singing. Youths raise their arms in a gesture of good omen, girls reel, and as the Nile floods the bosoms of dancing girls heave up and go down. Blessings abound and heaps of lemons, tomatoes, and vegetables grow bigger in Souk Al-Kumur.

Lights of lanterns are extinguished. Electric generators have provided water pumps with electricity and nights of weddings are now very bright with electricity. In August 2003, natives of Al-Kumur are supposed to be delighted with electricity from Al-Jaili Refinery east of the Nile.

With electricity transiting Al-Kumur, it will receive two currents: the electric current and the Nile's current which quenches the thirst of the Desert. Both currents head eastwards. But currents of Al-Tarad and the sands head westwards. Amid waves, currents, and struggle of the Nile with the Desert, Souk Al-Kumur disperses spices of luxury on commodities of poetry. Wisdom dangles as hair braids and poetry flows as canals on tongues of members of tribes.

Chapter (9)
The Compass and Nile's Direction

The Nile heads northwards from Khartoum up to Al-Hugnah Village, where the 1st cataract at Jabal (mount) Al-Rawyan not far away from Jabal Al-Atshan. In this place a compass is formed in the nature of land from mountains and cataracts that turned the course of the Nile eastwards.

The compass points east towards Al-Kumur. The Nile's current follows the direction. The compass turned the water current as if the Nile has sprang anew. The current stabs the depth of land and heads eastwards fast and eager to meet the sand of the Desert.

This spring meets another desert spring from the east, from the Empty Quarter in the Arabian Peninsula. Its sands head westwards to enter Sudan and cuddle with the Nile.

The thirst sand waves coming from the east, meet the Nile's flood to irrigate the thirst Desert on the land of cataracts in northern Sudan.

If you pass through the Desert road that divides Al-Kumur into two parts, then the scene is pitiful. But the road that goes parallel to the Nile evokes you to feel hopeful. There are green patches, water, sands, and a stroke of soil on the people's bodies.

Earth plates moved deep down the land of Al-Kumur and produced the four galaxies: sand and mud; some people from the ancient history of Al-Bijrawiyah, Al-Naqa', Kaboshiyah; some of them from the fringes of Al-Hambouti, Al-Mirmeedah, Jarab, and Al-Areef; and some from the Nile. They came from all passes of life and joy of days.

The Nile grants life to its banks and plains of Wadi Al-Hawad, of the eastern Al-Naqa' heights. From Al-Sadah Mountains and Fangol heights valleys come down. The eastern and western slopes meet at the tip of Nasri Island.

Nasri, Wad Abdullah, and the rest of islands are the connecting lines between the two Nile banks till modern bridges are built and hanging electric cableways (teleferiques) are run with tourists over Al-Kumur's region.

Islands are inundated with water during the flood. They court the vast expansion of space and stars at the time of recession. Trees of Sesban, Al-Tarfa, and Al-Dahseer grow on heights of the islands. They loom after the flood and call for cultivation of Al-Hameesy and Al-Magd.

The Nile's summer current builds and protects edges of the islands. The current calms down and turbidity of water is eliminated after the rage and boredom. The season of turmoil comes along and the flood swallows islands once more. Seasons pass by and migration to the Desert commences.

Immigration from the Nile is an expansion of fertility. Water flows out, trees planted, babies born, clouds embrace in space, valleys roar with rain storms that go down the slopes and irrigate the galaxies of Al-Kumur with heavy floods one time from the Desert and another from the Nile.

The Nile floods and drives out inhabitants of the islands to the Desert. After sometime, drought and heat drive them back. In the journey back home the trouble of heat is eliminated. The arrow of the compass has become the instructor of the Nile to all directions to irrigate the Desert till it finally pours in the Nuba Lake.

The Nile's course and direction had changed. It entered a new region. Contours were not the only thing that changed, but concepts too so that facts, imaginations, and ideas between reality and fiction emerge.

Chapter (10)
Between Reality and Fiction
Tales and stories in Al-Kumur are Nilotic, where they abound in African imaginations, Desert ones, full of Arabism, or a mixture of both reality and imagination such as the tales of Fatima Anez (goat of) Al-Hambak.

Story of Saleem Abdulasaseem
Al-Asaseem trace back to their ancestor Assoom. Their name is linked in Al-Kumur with the story of Saleem. I am not sure whether it is a legend, child stories, or a real one that happened sometime ago.

The image of Saleem Abdulasaseem comes and goes in my mind. I have seen him in person and I now see him between reality and imagination. The tales neared the character of Saleem to reality. But undoubtedly he is a Nilotic reality!!

Between dusk and evening Saleem comes out from the Nile with wet clothes. His face and shape both human. He walks on two legs and sometimes on four. His body covered with hair except his face, palms, and soles of his feet. Mosquitoes swarm around him. He drives them away with his hands. He was quiet, peaceful, and hurts no one. As a result he was called Saleem. He smiles exactly like a human being.

Al-Shabaleel says he is a blend of human and ape. But members of Al-Asaseem say he works with them in farming. He is one of their slaves who works, eats, and drinks during the day. But in the dusk he goes down to the Nile, dives in it, and disappears all night.

Saleem is a Nile's creature who comes out in the morning and lives with Al-Asaseem in their farms. He practices one thing in disguise if he has the chance. He nurses on milk from goats of neighbors. Some people say he is a monkey. Elders swear that he is a human being who lives deep in the Nile.

The Kings - inhabitants of Al-Jabrab Village - say that Saleem appears in the dawn before sunrise and swims the Nile to Al-Asaseem land opposite to their waterwheels in Nasri Island.

Saleem disappeared for a long time after the migration of people from Nasri Island to Al-Kumur, after Al-Tasab - the flood of 1946.

Abdulmajid Al-Hasan Assoom built his house near Al-Kardab and Al-Shabaleel. Suddenly at sunset a cold wind blew from the Nile and Saleem, who grew older, appeared on two slim legs walking towards Al-Kumur. He sat down on a heap of stones between the house of Wad Malik and Wad Murad. Saleem smiled and turned about as if he found what he was searching for.

News of Saleem leaked and the people gathered. Hands extended to greet him. He extended his hands to greet two persons at a time. Abdulmajid Wad Assoom brought him food. Saleem left the group and started devouring the food. People took notice of him as he was weeping. They all wept with him!!

Hamad Wad Abdulraheem appeared protruding his chest out denying the news and looking for Saleem among the gathering. He made his way through the people with both hands and saying: "hey folks, move aside please. Is it true that Saleem has come?"

Hamad sat on the ground, put his hands on his head and said: "I Witness that No God except Allah and that Mohammed is the Messenger of Allah. Hey folks, this is Saleem himself. Oh folks hail the good days of Nasri Island and our waterwheels." He also wept. Hamzah Al-Malek patted on Hamad's shoulder and said: "Hamad hush! Bygones are bygones and they will never come back."

At dawn and before sunrise, Saleem slowly got down the rock as if he came out of it and started walking towards the Nile. People followed him. He turned to them shyly, smiled, and kept his sight to the ground.

Neighboring villages rushed to see Saleem. Al-Hassaniyah Arabs came from the slopes of Fangol Mountains. Inhabitants of Al-Galah (Castle) rolled down from their houses into Abu Hawiyah valley. Al-Ja'liyeen and Al-Jabrab rode their camels, horses, and donkeys followed by Al-Hawaweer. Inhabitants of Um Zor and Al-Tarjamiyah got down to Al-Kumur.

All the people headed to the gap of the Desert. Men, women, and children climbed up Al-Tarad and gathered at its summit. Saleem said goodbye to them, retreated backwards, and descended into the Nile. The people requested him to come back. He started to dive and come up and finally disappeared.

People said at that mysterious night that the moon was full with a wide circle that overwhelmed all parts of the earth with light. Around its halo there were colored lines of yellow, blue, and green.

At that year the Nile flooded as never before till it reached the stones that Saleem sat on. And water entered the Souk (market) and inundated it. It was a year of blessings, abundance, and prosperity in Souk Al-Kumur.

Saleem disappears for a long time and his arrival usually coincides with the last farmers' boat. He stays behind for some time and sits on the edge of Nile so that his body adapts to the air. News reaches Al-Kumur and the people expect him. He sits on his usual rock. Abdulmajid Wad Assoom brings him food as usual. Saleem used to disappear and show up and with him blessings fill the market or disappear.

Saleem said goodbye to the people who were silent for a while then headed for their homes crossing the sands of the valley. And stories continued.

Hamad Wad Abdulraheem said: "Hey folks, let us go. Saleem has walked away. Our road is not the same."

Wad Kindi: "this sea (Nile) is all mysteries and enormities."

Wad Kadak hawked to continue talking: "Wad Kindi, haven't you seen Wad (son) of Al-Mulook (kings) who has struck the crocodile with a sickle?"

Wad Babiya interrupted him by saying: "he has not struck with a sickle only. But Wad Al-Mulook has fetched stones from Al-Jabrab Village. Once the crocodile comes out of water on the Island the boy storms him with stones."

Wad Kindi: "Aha, now the crocodile has snatched him."

All replied: "Yes, by Allah."

Wad Kindi ended the story by saying: "those who had seen him said when the crocodile grabbed him and went deep in the water, they said the hands that raised the boy were hands of a human being!!"

Wad Kadak: "hey man, the creature that snatched the boy was doing that in retaliation."

The story reached an end when they entered the Village of Al-Kumur and the roads branched at Al-Kardab's well. Hamad Wad Abdulraheem went eastwards, Wad Kindi westwards, Wad Kadak proceeded along towards the Vehicles Road, and the village roads swallowed the rest of men.

Stories of Fatima Anez (goat of) Al-Hambak

Fatima was neither stout nor slim. Her height was beautiful and her steps were brisk, wide, and few if compared to her height. She was black with soft and long hair. When she speaks everyone is able to hear her. She was decent and wise.

She used not to turn about while walking and when she has to she stops and turns her whole body. All people wish to talk to her. If she swears with her two boys (Al-Bashir and Ali) it means the truth and end.

Ali and Al-Bashir were two boys among five girls. Three of these girls lived in the urban and two in Al-Kumur. President Nimeri hanged her grandson lieutenant colonel Ahmed Jubarah Al-Shala in Hashim Al-Ata's military coup.

Since I first saw her, she was wearing a white clean Thobe (a Sudanese sari-like cloth) and tying a red handkerchief around her neck. Those two colors increase the power and wisdom of her character and present her as a fighter and one of the granddaughters of the Arab famous female poet Al-Khansa.

Fatima used to mock but not laugh. Her speech among Al-Kumur's community was constructive. She used to guide girls and glorify deeds of gallant men. When she loves something, she praises it very much and when she hates something she mutters with a low voice that increases her dignity and power of character.

Fatima also used to say her opinion clearly. One of her grandsons showed a desire to marry. She was not satisfied about the girl he wanted to marry. She told him after she murmured and a flood of words came out of her mouth: "Aha, when she sleeps, she slavers and when she tours the village, she stays long as if in a nap." He dismissed the idea of marrying that girl.

Fatima had a very beautiful daughter and there was a young handsome youth in Al-Kumur called Wad Malik who married one of the daughters of Zainab bint (daughter)

Hamzah who was a neighbor of Fatima. Fatima put the event in poetic words: "A'isha my daughter, who resembles the bottle on the *shelf*. Of bint Hamzah folks, the kite snatched her *kaf* (the sound of snatching). '*Kaf*' is used here to rhyme with *shelf*)."

Fatima left for Khartoum to visit her children, for medical treatment, spend days of Eid (feast) among her married daughters and boys by moving from one to another. She was moving among them according to their requests. All requested her for her sweet talk and wisdom. At twelve o'clock (midday), a goat bleated at a corner of the courtyard. Fatima remembered Al-Kumur and said to her daughter-in-law:

"Please my daughter; give this goat something to eat."

Her daughter-in-law: "he will come at two o'clock and will bring her clover with him (she meant her husband)."

Fatima murmured poetically: "Oh Allah, (*Al-Zain*) the Graceful, even the goat is waiting for (*Athnain*) the two o'clock."

Hamad Wad Rahamah said to Mohammed Wad Jubarah: "have you heard of Anez (goat) Al-Hambak in Khartoum?"

Mohammed Jubarah: "the truth is that she does not mean the goat. She means herself."

Hamad Wad Rahamah: "no, my brother, Fatima wants to be in her house; eats and drinks as she wishes."

The movement of Fatima among her daughters or sons-in-law takes her to her different present and makes her recalls the old memories written on the walls of her house in Al-Kumur. She felt eager to go home and begged her daughters and sons to let her go home.

Her sons and daughters were eager to host her, but that was useless. She couldn't forget Al-Kumur. It was impossible!

Fatima longed for Al-Kumur - that precious pearl in a necklace of sand and water, covered with the Desert's color, and glowed with the Nile's blue into green and yellow!!

Poet Al-Jahoori said: "Oh how eager I am to the distant Al-Kumur. Its fire increases sentiment. In the end I send greetings to Al-Turkey, the wooden board, Maseed (where he memorizes Holy Koran on a wooden board), and to everyone who asks about me. My greetings are sincere and they are all pure love. Soon I will see you Al-Kumur. Oh Nasri, laugh for me a lot."

The heat of the sun dropped down and the Nile's breeze rolled up the last of the Desert's simoom (hot wind). It was five o'clock p.m. and a group of people were in front of Abbas's shop for different purposes. Some were waiting for buses and trucks from east and west.

Abbas Wad Al-Hidai stood up to fill the ewer from the array of large jars in front of the shop. Rolled up his Damoriyah (cotton) shirt with his thumb and the forefinger to the middle of his chest and said about the heat:

"thank Allah, He cooled it a little! It was about to swallow us."

In front of the shop there were also women from Hajer Al-Tair (mount of birds) Village came to offer their condolences in Al-Kumur and waiting for the bus coming from Shandi. School pupils were smoking and discussing the football match between Hilal (Crescent) and Mireekh (Mars) teams. Elders were enjoying listening to the radio where Dr. Abdullah Al-Tayyeb was explaining the Sura (chapter of the Holy Koran) of Al-Nazea't while Sheikh Siddiq Ahmed Hamdoon was reciting. Girls around the well were filling their tins hurriedly so that bus passengers could not see them.

The buss stopped as an iron cage and opened its doors and her Thobe (a Sudanese sari-like cloth) flapped like the wings of a caged bird finally released. Fatima got down of the bus as a drowning person rescued by waves that drove him to the Desert's sand.

Fatima said: "Al-Kumur is the land of security." And added: "I ask Allah forgiveness, salute to you men." All were in front of Abbas's shop.

Abbas said: "hello my aunt Fatima, how are the folks there in Khartoum?"

Fatima: "thank Allah, they are all right. Come in the shop and give me a pound of sesame oil in a nylon bag." Then she uttered a couple of words only: "how is Al-Kumur?"

Abbas: "secure and safe."

The oil bag swung in her hand, she grabbed it with two fingers, and went out of the shop.

Fatima: "bye, may Allah take care of you!"

With wide strides she passed over the threshold, easily forgot the trouble of the journey, and stretched her body in the street heading towards her house with the hand bag on her left hand and the oil bag on the right.

After passing the corner of the shop, a cold wind of the shadow, she knew best, touched her face. It was the fragrance of homeland. She muttered the word of Al-Kumur.

The keys of the outer door, room, and other keys were all tied to her Thobe (a Sudanese sari-like cloth). She attacked the outer door. The goats jubilated a lot in the house of her daughter Faraheen (means double joy) and bleated high heralding her arrival. What amazing was that the goats did not see Fatima, but something happened!

Fatima stretched her tall physique in the middle of the courtyard and inspected its corners. The array of large water jars was empty for a long time. She headed towards the room, opened the door, looked upwards more than downwards, and counted important things hanging on the ceiling. The rain did not destroy them.

Fatima lifted Al-Angaraib (wooden bed) to her right side and hugged the pillows as if she was hugging a deer and beloved person. The bed was rectangular shaped with high legs. It becomes a trapezium when you move it, but returns back to the rectangular shape when it settles down on the ground.

Its legs were not decorated with geometrical shapes only, but also with time old stories.

Fatima got into the house again and looked at the packs of the rolled Damour (cotton clothes) and straw mats tied with ropes made by Al-Tarshan (the deaf). How many straw mats, ropes, cushions have worn out and the bed is still there!! She changed its left leg and tied another with a strip of a cow's hide.

She spread the straw mat and fetched an oil-smeared pillow. She took the blue two-surface table. The lower surface of the table was made of one piece of wood where she put her snuff box. She poured the oil in a pot, changed her clothes, poured oil on her hands and started anointing her body.

The outer door moved and a ten years old girl came in after hearing the movement in the house. "My grandmother has arrived!" She returned back hurriedly from one house to another. "Al-Busharah (prize for the good news) Al-Busharah, my grandmother has arrived." News spread with the evening dreams.

Her daughter Faraheen stretched out her neck over the neighbors' wall and told her other sister. Her sister called her neighbor and thus news spread farther. The doors moved, goats bleated, and her daughter came in rushing and pulling half of her thobe (Sudanese sari-like cloth) on the ground. A throng of children were jumping in the middle of the courtyard with candy papers flying up from their hands. "My grandmother has arrived! My grandmother has arrived!"

The girls with successive voices: " how are you, mother?" they came towards her with their bosoms and hands opened to hug her. They took turn in hugging and greeting her.

Faraheen to her mother: "you have opened the door and took out the bed? You are also anointing!!"

Fatima poetically: "hey girls, the oil is mine and the house is mine too. I am free to do with them. No *Karkabah* (noise) and no one will say I stained the *Martabah* (the mattress)."

One of her granddaughters slept at her feet, behind her there was a child, and another granddaughter of her second daughter was on the other bed. Nevertheless, Fatima slept profoundly.

Fatima was happy with her dreams, swam with Ursa Minor and Major (Little and Great Bears), wandered with ostriches, chased horses, lead the galaxy road fearing scorpions, and the aster came to her with the morning tea.

All around her laughed. In that winter day news spread farther in Al-Kumur as a light rain. Al-Haid told Al-Hawad, Al-Na'oom heard, and news spread.

Echoes of Fatima's story overwhelmed Fangol, Al-Azozab, Al-Ja'liyeen Village, Al-Jabrab, Al-Tarjamiyah, and Galat (Castle) of Al-Bakriyah. When they mention her name, they all remember her past tales and end saying: "thank Allah, she came safe."

Hamdeen narrates to the gathering of Al-Tarjamiyah one of Fatima's tales, and Taiallah imitates her voice and gait. They all laughed and one of them said: "hey man thank Allah, she came safe." In Um Zor the girls of Al-Sha'it also said: "thank Allah, she came safe."

Hamad Wad Rahamah and Mohammed Jubarah entered the coffee shop and restaurant of Hasabalrasool in Souk Al-Kumur for breakfast.

Hamad: "Please two dishes of beans with more oil on them."

Hasabalrasool: "oil of Anez (goat) Al-Hambak."

They all laughed and quoted Fatima's words: "The oil is mine and the house is mine too. I am free to do with them. No *Karkabah* (noise) and no one will say I stained the *Martabah* (the mattress).

Marriage of the Female Jinn
He chose to live in the Desert and leave Al-Kumur's community. He used to move with

the big flock of sheep, rides a camel, and carries his luggage on a donkey. Abu Ali Wad Al-Kateer does not go down to Al-Kumur except for shopping.

Do some people get married from female jinni? Does marital life become natural between them in interaction and sex?

He was known as Wad Al-Kateer, but nicknamed Abu Ali. He was a member of Al-Tarjamiyah Village. He settled in the north western side of Al-Kumur Village beside Um Zor after he surpassed forty five years of age and built a house for him. He got married for the second time and started to make a family of human beings.

His first jinni wife was still chasing him. He alone could see her and no one else. After he married his second wife, the jinni wife vowed to retaliate. She destroyed every thing he owned: the sheep and sumpters, and used to come to him for a moment while he was awake or asleep.

He was a good and timid man who used to walk quietly and focus his sight on the ground. He used not to hug people when greeting them as Al-Kumur's people do, but extend his hand for greeting as Bedouins. He was always near to you with his heart at the moment of greeting. He used to smile slowly and was neither tall nor short. He was slim and slanted a little forward.

He did not like to tour Souk (market) Al-Kumur. He used to sit leaning his back to one of the shop's pillars, survey with his sight all corners of the market and passers bye, stand abruptly, put his hands behind him, and walk out of the market.

Wad Al-Kateer used to perform light works in the market. He perfected painting houses from inside and transporting the colored soil in Eids (feasts). He had one goat for milk. The people of land and sea (Nile) were in the past days speaking about his big flocks of sheep.

Some one met him in the market, agreed with him to paint a room, and asked him about a color that inclines to orange. Wad Al-Kateer replied smilingly and precisely:

"it is there in Fangol Mountains." He fetched that color, mixed it with water, and told the client that he would come to him after two days.

Wad Al-Kateer used to work quietly as if observing something going around him. I came with food at mid day, put it before him, and asked him loudly:

"Oh, Abu Ali I want to ask you a question?"

Abu Ali: "why not son! I don't mind." And by his laughter I knew his absolute approval. We talked together about a fight that had occurred on last Monday in the Animals Market.

He said to me: "but you have not asked me?"

I said to him: "is it true that you were married to a jinni?"

He said: "yes, by Allah my son. Our time has now elapsed. That was in the early days when I was young."

I asked: "how?"

"I was young, owned a lot of animals, and used to shepherd them alone in the countryside. A female jinni used to come to me after twilight. She was beautiful as normal girls with a fair skin and black long hair. Her fingers were thick and long as if they had never touched something. Her face was white, cheeks bright, and a fistful thin waist.

She used to come to me from the direction of the wind, perfumed with Khumra (a Sudanese female fragrance composed of a mixture of many perfumes left in a bottle for some days to ferment), other sprinkling perfumes, had a smoke sauna of good-scented Talh and Shaf woods, massaged, and decorated hands and feet with black henna (camphire)."

He then cleared his throat and said: "Oh, boy her appointments were exact and known. She used to lie beside me and we were man and woman till the morning."

Groups of his tribe - inhabitants of Al-Tarjamiyah - tracked him down, waved to him to get down and live among people, and get married. They overcame him and convinced him.

He said: "the female jinni threatened me, vowed that if I left her she would show me woes in subsistence, children, and in myself. She wept and threatened when I left her. Every morning I found five of my animals dead. Gradually I lost them all."

He paused for a moment and said: "Before killing the animals, she used to utter some verses of poetry, I forgot them now! Any way with verses of the Holy Koran and religious and good people I managed to marry and live here. She used to come day after another, sit on the wall, and weep."

"Weeps at your house in Al-Kumur?"

"Yes, at this well-known house of mine."

Wad Al-Kateer had married a very tall and good physique polite woman. All neighbors spoke well about her. She knew rights of neighborhood, participated in occasions, and did her best to be nice with women in Al-Kumur and neighboring villages.

Wad Al-Kateer and his wife were blessed with two boys and a daughter. The daughter married when she was eleven years old and left with her husband. The elder son Ali was fond of football. He and his younger brother made their best to help their father make the family happy.

The flock of animals started to drop one after another!! People knew the cause and they were no longer amazed. Rumors started to circulate in Souk Al-Kumur.

Mohammed Wad Jubarah: "hey guys, have you heard of the tale of Wad Al-Kateer's goats and sheep?"

Hamad Wad Rahamah: "May Allah help them?"

Ali Wad Siddiq lifted his right leg up on the couch of the coffee shop: "Oh folks, this female jinni will not leave them."

Faraj Wad Al-Huwar: "I think they have to look for a Faki "religious man" to release them of this misfortune."

Hamad Wad Rahamah: "these folks deserve a help. This means we have to include them in the care and aid list."

Hamad and his group usually take care of the concerns and worries of inhabitants of the village.

The flock of sheep and goats gradually decreased and finally there was no goat to milk even for tea. Ali, the elder son, started frequently complaining from a fever that was quivering him. He died at the age of twenty, his brother followed suit in the same age, then the father and mother after some time.

The whole family tree fell off with its fruits in a cemetery beside the Nile. As fruits fall off a tree on a lake, small ripples come out on the surface. These circles grew wider and wider and finally fade away and fruits plunged deep in the lake.

Wad Al-Kateer house remained on the edge of Al-Kumur Village. People abandoned it due to tales about the retaliating female jinni. When people pass by the house, they recite verses of the Holy Koran and curse jinn.

Butchers' noise grew louder in Souk Al-Kumur and a hurly-burly outside the market mixed with bleats of goats in the Animals Market. Hajah bint Zainaldeen's house filled and emptied from both elder and young people. Students congregated around the sewing machine of Ali Wad Sineen and a number of farmers followed the merchant Ali Bashir for a loan and prepayments against future crops, as farming season was about to advent.

Floods of people entered from the five gates of the market. Al-Sir Wad Al-Ijaimi stood in the center of the market moving his head briskly and said: "where are these people going to?" he answered his question by saying: "yes, by Allah they are going to the Monday's market."

Chapter (11)

Souk Al-Kumur

Souk Al-Kumur was built by the British in the colonization era. It is now a center of circle of villages around Al-Kumur. Floods of people come into it from neighboring villages every morning throughout the week. Numbers increase on Thursdays and Mondays (market days). Abdulfadeel said: "Friday is once a week but the market is twice."

Buses and trucks come in early morning to transport passengers and unload commodities. They head west towards Omdurman or east towards Shindi along the Nile course. Lines of journeys are written on buses i.e. Al-Kumur – Omdurman, Al-Kumur- Shindi, Al-Kumur-Bahri and vice versa. Other sentences like: "may Allah pierce the eye of the envier with a stick", "beautiful and well-decorated, I adore it!", "show us and drive here and there," "Oh, the Most Kind, Allah", and "May Allah protect it," are also written on buses.

As birds come down and pick their blessings, buses also collect their passengers when neighboring villages send out their men.

Many come from behind Fangol Mountains. They sleep in the sand of Wadi Abu Hawiyah so that they could enter the market early in the morning. They carry fruits, dates, and various types of vegetables. A man brings with him he- or she-goat. Another uses the saddle of his sumpter as a pillow and presents before him bottles of native ghee, chicken, cocks, and hens.

Riders of donkeys, camels, or oxen and pedestrians hurry to enter the market. Women carry on their heads and shoulders commodities for sale. A group of men sitting on the back of a pick-up truck swaying to keep balance and one passenger snatches the turban of another and gives it to a third one. The speed of these vehicles is almost the same and passengers exchange conversations and jokes along the journey to the market.

Lines of conversations are open and deliberations about profit and loss are on full swing. Passengers also brag about the commodities they carry to the market. Running children carry chickens for sale. Young girls carry caps, handkerchiefs, and enter the market from the flour mill's gate. Others enter from the bakery's gate.

Inlets and gates of the market tell about the echo of generations. Roofs of shops are built from trunks of palm trees and branches. Walls are overhauled from inside with Desert's sands. There are thick mud pillars buttressing verandahs. They are unlike the pillars of the Romans or Greeks, but from the glorious history of Sudan.

On the edges of shops there appear the erosion of floods and on the walls the erosion of pouring rains. The market is not washed away by rain storms, but worn out through time. It looks antique as if it is the ruins of A'd's era.

If you enter the market after sunset when it is empty, the silence and the distant past din into your ears. At the morning rush, you hear jargons, songs, and tales as a traditional song before the eras of Dowbait (two-versed Sudanese poems).

Some stores bear names like "sold" and "bought" in old eras, such as Al-Bathani, Wad (son of) Al-Libaih in the Dates Market. "Al-Dabi Wad Siraj and Haj Al-Sheikh for Haberdashery"; "Wad Adam" and "Wad Babiyah" in the Spices Market; "Mahmoud Wad Saeed and Musa Wad Sulaiman for Trade and Agriculture"; "Awad and Himaid" in the Vegetables and Fruits Market"; "Awlad (sons of) Bashir Wad Hamid for Whole and Retail Trading " in the middle of the market"; "Wad Kasir", "Wad Sha'r Al-Bal," and "Musa Wad Al-Asad" in the Butchery.

Musa the butcher shouted "Al-Waga (2 ¼ kilos) of meat for one Riyal". Al-Hasan Wad Al-Asad here said: "Musa has jargoned." Those sitting under Al-Kardab palm trees in Nasri Island heard him shouting.

The talks and shouts of the crowd mix in the square of vegetable traders with jokes of barbers, tailors, and chaotic talking of butchers. During selling and buying you hear the snapping of shoemakers and blacksmiths.

Members of Al-Sawardah are famous of iron treatments. Awald (sons of) Abu Suwar has inherited the smithery from their forefathers. It goes deep into the clattering of Al-Bajrawiyah iron heaps near Kaboshiyah at the River Nile. And in the Arabian Peninsula Al-Waleed bin Al-Mugheerah was a blacksmith, (reference Al-Mahasin Wad Al-Adhadh "Merits and Opposites" book page 93).

The native ghee and types of threads are presented timidly in the Women's Souk (market), where some sort of courtship is practiced. Guffaws and laughter are louder in the coffee shops and restaurants.

Brokers and peddlers abound in the Vegetables and Fruits Market. A peddler calls for this commodity, buyers roam the market, chanters of praise poems to Prophet Mohammed (PBUH) keep on extolling, and a grandchild follows his grandfather in the Women's Market. Saleem comes out shyly, as a result the market flourishes, and high she-camels are heavily loaded.

Buyers scramble on heaps of various vegetables. Bint (daughter of) Saad, an old woman, scrambled with a group to buy vegetables. During the scrambling she fell on her knees. Qurashi Wad Nafeea, poet of Wedi Al-Qubah, was watching from a distance. He said poetically: "the anger and frustration, which till now I remember, was because the boys pushed bint Saad over the raw food."

Tales of Souk Al-Kumur have three aspects: real, fiction, or something between real and fiction. Tales and poems circulate inside and outside the market. Brokers' and drivers' tales are the ones between real and fiction. They are found inside and outside the market.

The tales inside the market are those of merchants, butchers, smiths, barbers, coffee boys and vegetable sellers. The tales outside the market are those of the court, slaughterhouse, Animals Market, donkey shavers, and house of Hajah Bint Zainaldeen. Brokers play on the two ropes (sides) i.e. outside and inside the market (so that, as the proverb goes, not to come out of the market with neither chicken pea nor flour).

Wheat is ground in mills, which overwhelm the market with noise till you could hardly hear anything and language changes into signs. It is kneaded, patted, and baked in bakeries in all corners of the market.

Stories of mills and bakeries end at four a.m. when bread trays come out of bakeries and Baker Siddiq Wad Abdulseed sleeps with some flour on his eyelashes.

Commodities come to Souk Al-Kumur from the west, from Omdurman; east, from Shandi and Berber; south, from across the Nile from Al-Butanah, Bahri (Khartoum

North), and Rufa'ah. From north come smuggled commodities across the Desert through Al-Arbaeen (forty days) Road between Egypt and Sudan.

In the stores over the shelves Sudanese sari-like thobes: Abu Gigaigah, Travera, Bangali, and Ganjah are displayed. Mouths of date sacks are closed; tins of Tahniyah, tahini (thick sauce made of sesame oil), and cotton seed and sesame oils are opened; and basins are filled with Harjal (herb), fenugreek, and Al-Mahraib (aromatic desert herb).

When you enter Souk Al-Kumur you are shocked with the smell of spices coming from Sind region in India, expensive perfumes of aloes (wood), Talha, Shaf, Kilait, and sandalwood; plus mahlabiyah (extract from mahaleb), Saratiua (pennywort), Majmua, and dyes for bed sheets and straw mats.

At the gates, edges of Swiss white textile, Sacobace (light linen), Solar, Ganjah (thick linen), and Damour (thick cotton fabric) flapped. Girls of Wadi Khalil weave red and green caps and hang beside them desert-colored Hijaz scarves. On the thin threads in front of the shops types of padlocks, chains, and safety pins are exhibited.

With a pyramid-like heap we find original henna of Al-Damer. There is also the British two-lion mark honey. Words like imported from Kenya, Ceylon, India, and Pakistan, are written on tea packs.

The inside corners of the market are decorated with colored durra mountain-like heaps such as Al-Mugd, Humaisi, Um Baneen (sometimes called Fataritah) that come from rain irrigated projects in Al-Qadarif and loaded on trucks of Wad Fatootah and Al-Tahir along with tales of Al-Butanah plains. But Wad Tola, the driver's helper, in the truck of Wad Abrain, has specialized in bringing Wad Amari (Sudanese snuff) from western Sudan.

The dried venison and ghee come from Jarab, Al-Areef, Al-Hambouti, and Al-Mirmeedah. Trade has nothing to be ashamed of, (Abu Sufian bin Harb was selling oil, hides (the reference is Al-Mahasin and Al-Adhadh "Merits and Opposites" book of Al-Jahiz, page 93).

Shuwain, Wad Jufoon, and Wad Al-Zain were from the rural Arabs who became rich. Each one of them was tying sixty camels as quiet sumpters with the tail of each camel in front of the nose of the other. Each camel was loaded with one and a half ardeb of durra (three sacks) from the stores of Hajj Mohammed, Mahmoud Wad Saeed, and Haj Salwah; at the time when durra was measured by sacks and oil with Mintal.

The sun is now in the middle of the sky and its heat overwhelmed the circle of the market. Shadows are now under the pillars of verandahs and the dazzling light crept to the thresholds of shops.

Various odors spread from the cotton seed moth, oil tins, and Tahniyah. A mouse chased its young female under the spice sacks in the shop's corner.

Most merchants stood on the doors of their shops hunting for a breath of air against the simmering summer heat and Desert's simoom, and watching Musa the butcher!!

The heat of stores suffocated merchants who did not enter their stores unless there was a client. And even then with a sigh or two of grumbling. "Pooh!! Hey people, what a heat?"

Babiker Wad Babiya sneezed in the spice store and came out hurriedly. "This is the summer season and the Pleiades are out."

Musa the butcher stroke the remaining meat with his hand and held the knife in preparation. He had to get rid of the meat!! He shouted and reduced the morning price. "Come on, come on, it is now free!!" A moment and the merchants scrambled. They were perfectly aware of this moment.

Fast and before merchants arrive he pushed away three of the sheep's heads. He would clean them fast and neat for himself. Merchants evacuated the tray from the rest of meat and bellies. He expelled flies and put the sheep's heads into his Damour (cotton) bag. He looked at his arm and said:

"by Allah, the hair of my arm rose up!!" he blew the back of his hand and said: "cool down!!" Spat on

his palm, rubbed his body, and said: "Oh Allah, protect me from the eyes of people."

"It has gone down!" "The sun has gone down." "Here I am coming Um Zain." He turned his back and revolved half a circle. Flies followed and landed on the Aluminum-coated meat table. With a dance he put down his apron from his waist, sang, and hummed: "thousand greetings from me to her. Oh beautiful with a live feelings. She lodges in Al-Awadiyah; hob, hob, Oh people, Oh people!!"

He chanted with a loud, beautiful, and husky voice; leapt twice in the air and hit the ground with his foot.

Al-Hasan Wad Al-Asad faced him. They jumped and landed in harmony. Their voices matched. Wad Al-Sha'r Al-Bal rose up and got between them saying: "you made us remember the days of youth. Glad tidings to you! The end of a human is a heap of soil."

Musa: "goodbye and May Allah protect you pals. See you on Thursday." Musa used to come from Wad Al-Habashi Village to Souk Al-Kumur every Monday and Thursday. "Friday is once, but the Souk (market) is twice!!"

Every merchant used to have a shop with warehouses behind it. Some professions were being practiced in front of the shops. Sheikh Al-A'lim Al-Turky was at first a tailor in front of his brother Mahmoud's shop. (Abu Hanifah was also a silk dealer. The reference is Al-Mahasin and Al-Adhadh "Merits and Opposites" book, page 93).

Trucks unload different types of durra in sacks, which is winnowed, sifted, sorted out, and heaped. Its pyramid-like heaps stand up in the northern part of the market where goats fiercely attack them.

Zainab bint Hamzah has a goat which used to lurk intelligently at the eastern gate of the market. Thus it is able to see all mountain-like heaps of durra in the northern part. It scratches its right side on the wall while lurking, then suddenly attacks the first durra mountain-like heap before it is expelled. Once again it pokes its nose in the second heap, before a shower of stones drives it away. It jumps into the third heap, receives a strong blow, and falls on its right side in the fourth heap. Thus it continues devouring durra. It finally shakes itself and exits the market through the western gate at the Animals Market and house of Al-Hajah bint Zainaldeen.

Haj Salwah laughed and said: "be ready for the second attack." Fathallah replied: "May Allah kill this naughty goat and seize its coming from the western part of the market."

Noise of gristmills change when wheat or durra is no longer there and roar again when full. The fine grist goes down and the roar of gristmills mixes with the noise of sewing machines in the shops of Al-Amin and Ali Wad Sineen.

The British chose the site of Souk (market) Al-Kumur very carefully. They drew a map that resembled the British flag. If you look from above, the bakery of the Sheikh of the Line (of village) is in front of the court and the flagpole. The colors are different. There were two colors only in the flag that represent the Nile and Desert, where the Arabs of the banks tour.

The British wanted to leave their imprints on all things. They built the Palace of Gordon Pasha, the General Ruler of Sudan, meters away from the River Nile so that the Nile flows under his feet. The Mahadiyah dervishes killed Gordon and the Palace was turned into the Republican Palace.

Engines of Amjad Factory, for Sudanese automobile industry, keep on running and the streets of Khartoum are crowded with Japanese and German cars.

The shops in Souk Al-Kumur resembled pieces of a necklace coming down the chest of the Desert and into the Nile's bosom. Souk Al-Kumur at that time was the second biggest market on the western bank of the Nile after Souk Omdurman.

Silk was imported from Kashmir, rice from Thailand, clothes from Bangladesh, and batteries from Poland and Holland. Radios in coffee shops and stores transmitted different broadcasting frequencies from London (BBC), Mont Carlo, and Omdurman. Mohammad Wardi, the famous Sudanese singer chanted: "oh my longing heart. Why he antagonizes you and you don't!!" It was a time of sincerity and yearning.

Men of Wad Keer, including Al-Dager, were used to come to the market with their thoroughbred and known donkeys; Jadallah Wad Sheikh Ali with his camels, and Yuobi on his horse from Hajer Al-Tair (mount of birds). The turban was a symbol of elegance and the scarf a symbol of Sheikhdom.

The British divided the market into two squares and six entrances. The butchery was sited in the middle of the first square. The shades of porters and smiths, and vegetable and fruit tables were in the second square.

The Animals Market was outside the market and west of sheep and oxen slaughter place on the stones of the slaughterhouse. The camels' kneel- down spot was to the east and the horses and donkeys' stall was to the south. (Al-A's bin Wa'il used to treat horses and camels. The reference is Al-Mahasin and Al-Dhadh "Merits and Opposites" book, page 93).

Some rich people of big cities like Shandi acquired their wealth from Souk Al-Kumur. Al-Tayyeb Haj Mohammed had a shop, bakery, and stores for crops. Mohammed Ahmed Taha had a pump for irrigation of the agricultural lands in Nasri Island and crop stores in the market. Hussein Abdulmajid and his brother Atalmanan and Mahmoud Saeed jointly had a shop, restaurant, and coffee shop. They moved with their moneys down the stream to Shandi market.

Some Customs of Tribes inside and outside the Market

The Arab-Nilotic tribes – Al-Ja'liyeen and Al-Shaygiyah - mix in the region of Shandi, east and west. These tribes are cousins; in addition to Al-Hassaniyah tribe that lives cautiously on the banks of the Nile and tends to lead a nomadic and Bedouin life.

These tribes are daily found in Souk Al-Kumur. Every individual is at his specific spot as usual. Members of Al-Hassaniyah are cautiously found at the Animals Market, and inhabitants of the islands at the vegetable and fruit stores. The market is a scene for exhibiting customs and natures.

If a dispute arises between Al-Ja'liyeen and Al-Shaygiyah, and a member of Al-Shaygiyah came in. He does not ask about the cause of the dispute, but immediately sides with his fellow tribe member without questioning. But a member of Al-Ja'liyeen tribe is usually seen separating people, during the peak of a dispute, and sides no one. He asks about the cause of the dispute and opts to reconciliation and compromise.

If a misunderstanding arises between Al-Ja'liyeen themselves, they tend to hide it from others and you never hear about their differences until a long time elapses. But among members of Al-Shaygiyah tribe, voices are high and they don't care of being heard by others.

At congregations that entail traveling to courts outside Souk Al-Kumur, members of Al-Ja'liyeen tribe participate with few numbers for representation purpose only. But members of Al-Shaygiyah tribe scramble to travel and increase their number for the purpose of bragging.

Female members of Al-Ja'liyeen tribe tend to boast and show up their gold and inherited properties. They also show seriousness and power upon speaking. But female members of Al-Shaygiyah tribe joke a lot and tend to apply the proverb that says "pass away worries with joy and happiness."

Discussions abound in Souk Al-Kumur between members of Al-Shaygiyah and Al-Ja'liyeen tribes. They sit on the ground and draw lines with sticks during conversations. A member of Al-Shaygiyah tribe draws broad lines from right to left mimicking the tribal scars on his cheeks. But the member of Al-Ja'liyeen tribe draws lines from top to bottom as his tribal cheek scars. But if lines intersected from top to bottom and from right to left, then the people who drew them were a mix of both tribes. And all lines drawn inside a square would be an evidence for unity and kinship. Lines are still intersecting inside Souk Al-Kumur.

Members of Al-Hassaniyah tribe are peaceful and they always sell their commodities outside the market and buy their requirements that include salt and sugar. They ride their donkeys and hit the defiles, valleys, and top of the mountains and say: "let bygones be bygones."

Jokes in Souk Al-Kumur

The butchers are the source of jokes and tales of the market. Al-Hasan Al-Asad sat in front of Mahmoud Wad Saeed's shop with elders of the market which include Omdah (Mayor) Bushara, Taj Al-Sir Bashir, etc., speaking about incidents occurred in the court.

Awad, son of Al-Hasan, passed in front of them hauling a long stick and wearing a red cap that covered his eyebrows. His father clapped his hands to draw the attention of the group. The group attended and listened.

Al-Hasan Al-Asad: "listen men, I swear (by the divorce my wife) in this life nothing amazes more than the crazy youthful deeds of my son Al-Awad!!"

The group astonished for tackling a different subject, wondered, laughed; and paid attention to his son Al-Awad who looked youthful and challenging. Al-Awad appeared as if saying" I am not a member of your group and I don't care a damn."

Al-Hasan stood up and Mayor Bushara directed stingy words to him as he was heading towards the butchery.

Awad Al-Asad grew up with an intelligent, frolic and somewhat chaotic character. When you sit with him you ask for more and more jokes, descriptions, and imitations to others. He reincarnates characters cunningly and confidently. He enters areas of rich talking and knows how to come out of them jokingly and without embarrassment, because of his high dose of daring that almost nears indifference.

He acquired his daring character from his experience in the army where he was a parachutist. He reduces a long story into few words as if coming down with a parachute. Calculations of time in the air, between loss of life and landing, acquired him fast deliberation and quick results.

Awad Al-Asad, from the first sight, knows when you speak to him what you intend to hide. He very oftenly says:" I got you!" When he disagrees with you he leaves you, because he does not want to mess things. He is pleasant and good natured. Joy always blocks sad areas in him.

Youth has ended in his peers and started in Awad. He wakes up with a frown and suddenly laughs. He rejoices day light and jubilates all day long as a sunflower.

The sun had set down and silence overwhelmed all corners of the market. Merchants started to collect their commodities and money as if a call from heaven said: "means of subsistence have now seized." Wad Al-Fadul used to guide people in Maghrib (dusk) prayer and they used to ask him to make it short.

People lined up for the dusk prayer, the Imam stepped forward and initiated prayer. Fathalrahman Wad Sha'r Al-Bal (wet hair) pulled the Imam and said: "he leads us in the prayer because he has a lot of money. I swear (by the divorce of my wife) I will lead you this time." He stepped forward and said: "Allah is the Greatest." All started praying.

After finishing prayer by saying: "peace be upon you all," they started to laugh quietly and giggled loudly. Fathallah Wad Karom stood up to leave and said: "By Allah, you have to repeat this prayer!"

Wad Sha'r Al-Bal replied: "why? What is wrong with it?" The group dusted off their shoes and dispersed.

Terms of the Desert appear in the butchers' tales in Souk Al-Kumur as they are closely related to the Animals Market in the north eastern part and Al-Hassaniyah tribe as they trade in animals. The relation extends to outside the market to Wadi Abu Hawiyah, Moshra' (berth) Abu Jamal (camel), Wedi (small wadi) Al-Qubah (dome), and passes of the Deserts.

Vegetable sellers' tales, in the southern part of the market, are an extension to the Nile's relation with Al-Karo, Um Bagarah (cow), and Nasri Island.

The Nile's products in Souk Al-Kumur are heaps of lemon, fresh fruits with different colors, dried dates including Al-Barakawi,

Al-Jaw; Molokhiyah (Jew's mallow), Saparoq, and leaves of cowpeas, ears of maize, okra, and Hinaiteer.

Tomatoes are the freshest soiled vegetables from the escarpments. They are heaped one over another or put in boxes. Tomato sellers shout: "look at it with you own eyes. It is delicious and local." They mean to warn you not to let anybody else select tomatoes for you. You have to touch it gently. The seller wants you to see the green leave at its back as a sign of freshness and an indication that it is just picked. Tomatoes usually brought to the market green with branches, not yet ripe, or full red - completely ripe. Farmers love to flirt and touch the completely ripe tomatoes in the farm where they sway on branches beautifully.

The buyer aided by the seller shoulders a box of tomatoes without examining them. Only when tomatoes water on his shoulder, the buyer is puzzled. Must he return tomatoes back, throw them away and wash his hands and face, or make a sauce out of them?

Competition is fierce between local and imported tomatoes. One seller on an elevation in the vegetable market shouts: "Tomatoes! Tomatoes! They are local from our slopes. Beware of the imported!"

Local tomatoes endure soil and heat, because they ripe under the sun of our country. If you put them in fridges or air-conditioned rooms, they will be fresher, more beautiful, and beneficent.

Imported tomatoes are exhausted by long journeys under very cool degrees of temperatures. As a result when they are taken out of fridges, their color and taste change. They do not live long because chemicals and fertilizers have spoiled them. So they are soft, watery, and no longer good except for the sauce exhibited on shelves.

He heard voices in the sky. Looked up and saw a flock of birds flying in the air in an open-based triangle shape flapping wings and following its leader towards the east.

The sun had set down or almost, and the color of the sky was like the bottom of a valley; a mixture of sand and mud. This is the time of serenity and glorifying Allah. Birds came back to their nests with full craws. These birds are not like the pigeons of expatriates.

The Coffee Shops and Restaurants
There are seven coffee shops in Souk Al-Kumur. They start with tea utensils and add cooking pots later to be a restaurant. Chairs and tables are painted green (a mixture of blue and yellow) without prior agreement between coffee shop owners. It is a natural expression about the Nile and Desert. Visitors of the coffee shops are groups of Bedouins changed into settled Arabs living on the banks of the Nile.

The slopes and escarpments provide Souk Al-Kumur with blessings of coffee shops and restaurants. Matar Wad Shindoq, was the first owner of a coffee shop. He was a member of Al-Shanadiq tribe living in Wadi

Al-Jiraif (small escarpment) that starts from Um Zor and extends eastwards till Jiraif (escarpment of) Al-Matamah.

From Jiraif Al-Khartoum came Hasabalrasool Mohammed Idris, owner of the complex that included a coffee shop, restaurant, and bakery. He used to make loaf known as Toasti (toast) loaf and funnily enough his wife was called Shabiana (we are sated).

Hasabalrasool had special amicability with the group of Tarjamiyah; Taiallah, Hamdeen, Ahmed Abu Safah, Fadul Al-Mola, and Awald (sons of) Al-Saqr (eagle). In his last days he got married to a second wife from them.

The third coffee shop was owned by Al-Nur, who was a son-in-law. At his time he started making beans with salads, a mode of collective breakfast which the group of Al-Tarjamiyah excelled.

Al-Kumur's group; Hamad Wad Rahamah, Mohammed Wad Jubarah, and Ali Wad Siddiq were used to take breakfast in the central room and use the store and verandah for drinking tea.

The teachers' group was used to take its breakfast at Ali Abdulmajeed's restaurant. He used to leave the restaurant's key for them. After they finish eating at mid nigh, they lock it and pay their debts at the end of month when they receive their salaries.

The fifth coffee shop was owned by Fadul Al-Molah Wad Al-Qaram jointly shared with Musa Wad Sulaiman. They were four lined shops with a gasoline fridge full of Pepsi Cola, Miranda, and lemonade.

Competition was fierce between the coffee shops of Ali Kosti and Mohammed Saleh Al-Yemeni. The first came from Kosti City, in central Sudan, and the other from Al-Hudaidah in Yemen. They showed wonders of creation and competition. Experiences came from Al-Jiraif Sharq (east escarpment), valley of Al-Shanadiq, Kosti, and Yemen. Voices of waiters were high promoting for delicious types of foods, barbeques, and drinks.

Radio frequencies were turned to various international stations. You hear newscasts and programs of "what listeners' request". Wardi, the famous Sudanese singer, signs *'Al-Qamar Boba Alaik Taqil'* (the crescent-like earning is heavy for you to wear), *Al-Gazelle Foq Al-Salam* (gazelles gathered over there in the acacia wood), and *Al-Jazera Um Baharan Hima* (the island of the overwhelming sea 'Nile').

Radios broadcast news in early morning and around the clock. Buses and trucks also come from east and west in the evening and unload commodities. Drivers and commission agents (Ali Dongla, Abu Sabandiyah, and Wad Ibrain) also spread joy in Souk Al-Kumur with latest jokes and talks of expatriates coming from Omdurman and Shandi.

A number of Al-Kumur's expatriates in the Arab Gulf countries in front of Al-Nur's coffee shop. Al-Nur asked: "Oh expatriates, how work is in Saudi Arabia?" Azhari: "by Allah, we tried everything. We worked in coffee shops, groceries, restaurants, and butcheries. We tried to sell vegetables with Bangladeshis.' He named all professions found in Souk Al-Kumur.

Abbas: "how are things with you Al-Nur?"

Al-Nur laughed: "we are all right, eating and drinking; and marry one, two, three, and four wives. Our children grow, educate, and we are all happy. All this is from Souk Al-Kumur.

One expatriate said: "by Allah, here in Sudan we tried everything they say has possibilities of investment. Some of us built shops; others bought land plots and buses. But all this did not succeed."

Hashim: "all this will not succeed unless you supervise your properties yourself."

Omar: "originally expatriates' money are flying as pigeons, people tame them and breed to them."

Othman: "hey man, the expatriate needs to put pigeons in one cage and retain the cage's key to himself so that pigeons breed, grow, and increase for him."

Abu Obaidah: "some pigeons do not breed. You can trade in them."

Qassim: "hey man, you can slaughter, barbeque, eat and fill your stomach, and sate others."

Sir Al-Khatem: "how good is satiety?"

Abbas: "Aha, how to collect pigeons; one in Al-Kumur, one in Khartoum, and another in nowhere?"

Hamad and Mohammed Wad Jubarah appeared suddenly. Hamad's chest heaved as a Nile's flood and Wad Jubarah was slim as a rain storm course.

Hamad Wad Rahamah: "hey expatriates, be careful. Keep an eye on your pigeons and don't let them fly."

Mohammed Ahmed Jubarah about to strike one of the expatriates: "catch your pigeons, don't let them fly."

Al-Nur: "hey folks, thank Allah for seeing you and coming home."

His vacation came to an end. He went back loaded with instructions, memories, and parcels. All were waiting for him. "To be delivered to so-and-so" was written on one of the parcels. He received the parcel and letters. Someone asked him about home and the folks.

"Come on get inside."

"How good is the time of chatting!!? Now I am going for a second half of the workday. Tomorrow the bachelors will come and spend all day with me. Please, come with them."

He got down the staircase carrying the parcel packed with nylon bag. Got into his car and before opening the letters, he took a handful of baked and salted watermelon seeds into his mouth. He tasted and smelled the odor of spices (fennel, coriander, etc) and peanuts. He moves after putting all watermelon salted seeds into his mouth.

"Oh Allah, how good is the smell of homeland?"

He heard the sound of peeling the watermelon salted seeds and tasted the salt. He imagined Al-Kumur for a while looking through the windscreen of his car. "Sands are yonder, these are the stones colored as seeds, and some of them are burnt." He went deep in imagining Souk Al-Kumur, the basins for presenting goods, and winked at the girls selling peanut and seeds. He remembered the house of his maternal and paternal aunts and started muttering songs of old games.

"*Shilailo wen rah akalo al-tomsah. Shelailo weno akalo al-dodo. Ho, lob, lob. Kam fi al-khat.* (Where is the bone gone? Where is the bone? The crocodile has eaten it. Ho, lob, lob. How many are in the line.)

"*amana alaik, tigatie idnaik. Mahin sitah wa sitten. Kadaban kadib.*" (Swear by faith that will cut your ears, aren't thy sixty six? No, they are not.)

"*Amana alaik, tigatie idnaik. Aren't they arba' wa arab? Shid wa arkab.*" (Swear by faith that will cut your ears. Aren't they four and Arabs? Yes, they are; saddle and ride.) He shouted victoriously and jumped in joy over the sands of Dahiyat Al-Qird (posterior of the ape).

He read the letters while lying on his back. He did not think of the many demands. His mouth was full of watermelon salted seeds. He toured the narrow room with his sight. It did not at all look like Al-Kumur's rooms or houses. He got up of bed and entered the kitchen. Put four spoons of bulk tea and said: "Cures the tea. Get lost, no Lipton and no tambourine!" He did not like packed tea in small bags.

The telephone rang and he shouted: "Yes, coming."

"Tea is ready; meat and boiled food are on the fire."

"You reminded me of the waiters of Al-Nur's coffee shop."

They spoke about the coffee shops and restaurants. Another group came in accompanied with the carrier of parcels.

Al-Sir: "hey folks, have you heard the story of the watermelon salted seed?

"What about it. Has it got into your throat?"

Al-Sir: "I wish it had killed me and buried in the graveyard of Wad Bari?

"Hey man, it smells peanut and fennel."

"Untie fennels (let us hear rumors). How are the folks in Al-Kumur?"

The apartment was full with groups of bachelors and cigarette smoke billowing around the air conditioner. Memories flooded and there were series of talks and conversations. Evening came and all prepared for more talking and chanting.

Allahjabo (Allah has brought him) came from Juba to fish beside the Nile. His game went deep into the sand. He aimed with his spear. The spear's blade dropped. He covered the spear's shaft with a cow's hide. The shaft was then turned into Okaz (a stick). He took it with his right hand and entered Souk Al-Kumur from the western gate.

The rain storm of the valley flooded carrying a sword-like knife. The knife went deep beside the Nile. The man took the Sikeen (knife) sheathed it, wore it up on his left arm, and entered Souk Al-Kumur from the eastern gate. They say: "knife is the daughter of swords and mud is the daughter of escarpments."

They embraced each other in the center of the Souk (market) and repeated: "Salam, Salam." (Peace be upon you, peace be upon you,) and went together to Al-Nur's coffee shop.

Abu Sikeen (the one with the knife) and Abu Okaz (the one with a stick): "Oh expatriates, peace is upon you."

"You are welcome."

Abu Okaz: "these folks, what flying pigeons do they have?"

Abu Sikeen: "they are themselves flying and expatriates!"

Abu Okaz: "hey Al-Nur, please, two cups of Banjigli tea, plain tea and more sugar."

Al-Nur: "ready for you. Drink (toast) it in the health of Sudan."

Abu Sikeen: "hey Al-Nur, please turn the radio louder." They all paused to hear the song of the Sudanese famous singer Mohammed Wardi that went: "oh my beloved country! You who wear the garment, female sari-like thobe, big garment (Jibah), a vest, a sword, and a knife. You, who wear Jibah and sword; and Okaz (stick) and Sikeen (knife). Oh you beautiful and good. Oh you beautiful and good."

Abu Okaz: "the Banjigli goes down the veins and removes fatigue. Oh expatriates; Oh you, the disease. Migrate and be expatriates at your cousins the Arabs. We expatriate only in our Sudan."

Abu Sikeen: "hey Al-Nur, please tea again, half half (comme ci comme sa)."

Abu Okaz: "see these people, how clean and polished?"

Abu Sikeen: "hush, do not speak about them. They are expatriates who sold the homeland, sold the Sudan cheap."

"How is that?"

"See leaders of separation in the south, west, and east all are from the expatriates."

"Those expatriates, may Allah protect us from their evil."

"Expatriation has erased homeland from their hearts."

"This is only one negative aspect of expatriation."

"There are many other negative aspects."

"Sudan is good; it can not be traded for other countries."

Abu Sikeen: "haven't you heard the story of the beautiful woman which got married to an expatriate? He left her an ugly guy to raise the goats and serve her. With the long period of expatriation the ugly guy fell in love with the woman."

Abu Okaz: "have they committed Harram (impermissible)? Allah forbids!"

"Yes."

They asked her: "why did you do that and your husband is handsome and good looking?"

She said: "length of remoteness, nights of sleeplessness, and nearness of pillows!!"

"Yes, by Allah, farness is all sleeplessness for both those inside and outside the country."

"Yes, by Allah!"

Abu Okaz: "the expatriate is like one who marries an ugly woman but extravagantly rich."

Abu Sikeen: "even if she has money as a rain, she is still useless.

Abu Okaz: "yes, by Allah my pal Abu Sikeen. What do people say about such a guy?"

Abu Sikeen: "it is not a matter of a guy marrying an ugly woman! There are some people who expatriated in countries where a woman marries woman!!"

Abu Okaz laughed till he sat down on the ground and said: "how is that? May Allah protect us from such things?"

"Hey man, it is even a man marries a man!!"

Abu Sikeen: "oh Allah, how can that be?"

"As I tell you, this is what's happening."

"May Allah protect us from the evil of those expatriates?"

Abu Sikeen: "hey man, let me say something to you. We are controlling all things. Let us make a demonstration, lead it, and let them go behind us. I will exit from the eastern market gate and you from the western one."

Abu Okaz: "you mean each of us must exit from the gate he entered the market."

Abu Sikeen:" Yes, exactly! And we must meet together at the house of Hajah bint Zainaldeen."

They all shouted and each exited from the agreed gates and met at the house of bint Zainaldeen. The tall, green (black), and bareheaded beautiful woman received them.

Bint Zainaldeen: "what is the demonstration about? Listen men, neither the eastern nor western market gates. We want it a Sudanese style."

They all applauded and hailed bint Zainaldeen: "you talk nice bint Al-Zain! You talk nice!"

Abu Sikeen and Abu Okaz whispering to bint Zainaldeen each in one ear: "get these expatriates inside and shut the door. Operate the strainer. Your Mareesah (liquor) is strong and intoxicate these people."

Bint Zainaldeen: "is this what you want seniors. I swear I will do that. Welcome show off people!!"

Abu Okaz: "hey Hajah, it is not show off, but the demonstration." The similarity in the Arabic word "Al-Mathaher" which means "show off" mislead Hajah bint Zainaldeen to think that it was "Al-Mothahara" which means "demonstration".

Bint Zainaldeen: "welcome the people of the demonstration." She muttered and said: "tonight you will see the stars of mid day."

The gourd, bowl, cup, and glass turned around them with liquor.

Abu Okaz: "look at these people of yours; they no longer differentiate between the gourd and the bowl."

Wad Abu Sikeen: "hush, allow them some minutes."

Abu Okaz: "expatriation has messed these people and lost their minds. Each time appears an expatriate and calls for separation of the north from the south. Why don't you call for your rights only?"

Abu Okaz and Abu Sikeen together: "separation? You insane people!"

They laughed together and said: "by Allah, they have no mind, thinking, or marrow!!"

Abu Okaz: "see your pals, they slept completely. These are the friends of Afo in China, and so-and-so in Holland and Poland." (In reference to the imaginary geographical visits they made to friends in these countries in elementary school.)

Abu Sikeen: "some of them are sleeping with their heads up, on their backs, or on their bellies."

Abu Okaz: "by Allah, they are laying down six and Arabs. They don't have one (taba) that will enter them paradise."

Abu Okaz: "let them asleep. Al-Kokaraj (evil creature in games and tales) will come to them after some time."

Abu Sikeen: "you and I let us play Al-Seeja and Al-Tab. Let us make these people of yours play tom tom."

Abu Okaz: "hey bint Zainaldeen; bring that tin here to drum it for them instead of Al-Dalookah (a Sudanese female drum)."

Abu Sikeen: "you mean *Al-Gairawanah* (tin). Have these people of yours scattered in all parts of the world till they reached *Al-Qairawan* (a famous Islamic city in Tunisia) and Danube? What is wrong with the River Nile? Poor people! They migrated to all places: *Doglum Al-Safaiyah wa Al-Qairawan* (drum tins to them). They do not know. Hey you insane, the Nile and Desert do not separate!!"

Abu Okaz: "they are sleeping. See how every one is opening his mouth and ear?

Abu Sikeen: "they missed dawn prayer. It is said that he who misses dawn prayer, the devil urinates (pees) in his ears."

Abu Okaz laughed and said in bad Arabic language: "No, No, my brother, shame on you. Leave this talk of Arabs." It seems that Abu Okaz (means the man with a stick) is non-Arabic speaking man, for he pronounced "brother" and the rest of the sentence badly.

Dawn is now clear and the morning sleep overwhelmed Hajah bint Zainaldeen. She stretched her body on the bed and opened her eyes on the daylight and said: "in the name of Allah, Most Gracious, and Most merciful. Hey people, am I awake or dreaming?"

Eyes of expatriates opened at the west part of the market, the court, slaughterhouse, house of bint Zainaldeen, and Animals Market. Some of them got up and entered the market.

The Role of Tailors

Ali Mohammed Al-Hasan (Ali Sineen) and Al-Amin Wad Al-Mubarak returned from Omdurman. Their fathers have sent them to learn sewing profession. They were telling people about Al-Qasiriyah (the place where all tailors are located in the Central Station in Omdurman).

Each of them procured a sewing machine and returned to Souk Al-Kumur. They used to put on a garment, shoes, and socks; and sit on their sewing machines with local and imported textiles around them. They opened their shops beside the old tailors such as Wad Al-Kurunki, Wad Umbokol, and a group of tailors from Wad Al-Habashi Village.

Ali Sineen and Al-Amin Wad Al-Mubarak excelled the sewing of scarves for the grooms, knitting of buttons, and Kasr Amoud Al-Jalaleeb (a column of additional decorative line of sewing beside the first one). They showed art in sewing Karshaleek (the front part of a garment; from the chest to the belly), collars, and Janah Um Jakco (a big garment with wide sleeves that resembles the wing of a big African vulture). They sewed school bags, flannels, and aprons for waiters.

Ali Mohammed Al-Hasan used to joke with Al-Nur when the pockets of his apron dangle with coins and paper money. He used to sing when Al-Nur passes beside him: "you are the smart who has two pockets. Who resembles you?"

The educated, teachers, school pupils meet at the tailors' shops. They discuss politics, football (soccer) and go deep into the Arabic language, poetry, or parsing. They speak fluent English, because at that time syllabuses were not arabized.

Ali Sineen used to talk to the gathering in English, which he learnt by practice. Some visitors of the market avoid the seasonal gathering of pupils and students. Ali acquired the skill of talking to both categories and pay for tea, cold drinks, and breakfast oftenly. He linked between generations with his language and charm.

All generations meet at the tailor Ali Mohammed Al-Hasan in the Eid (feast) days. They stay awake to dawn. Some of them used to sing, play cards, and chat. You may also find two guys remotely whispering about a serious subject.

Ali Sineen participates with each group and interferes in the right moments he knows best. He is the master of the situation and axis of all rings. He participates with a word or description that makes all people laugh and then shouts: "hey people, let us listen to this song."

Ali Sineen used to sing and compose. He was sensitive and expert in selecting beautiful words, tunes, and songs. He believes that music renews youth and treats some diseases. He oftenly says: "music removes pain."

When song music starts, he was the first to mention the poet, composer, and singer. He sings a complete verse before the singer starts it. He says: "these are the words of the Sudanese poet Idris Jamaa, and the composer and performer is Othman Hussein."

The words say: (You, the Nile, the descendant of paradises. Angles embraced you in eternal heaven, and flapped on you green wings.)

He interprets the green wing by saying they are the two banks of the Nile that retain the Desert. He also chants Abdulkareen Al-Kable's song: "my heart since I am born seduces girls. This time its pain is unbearable and the healer is unable to cure it.)

Ali had potential talents. He did not miss a comparison or description. He used to imitate his father and sister, and excelled in imitating his young brother teacher Ahmed. He perfected the art of addressing and courtesy in speaking. He was clean in his body, elegant in his clothes, and loved by his neighbors. He treated every old lady in Al-Kumur as his mother, every old man as his father, every young man as his brother, every child as his son, and every peer as a friend. All those mentioned above did not escape his comments. They understand him when he describes someone in particular.

Ali does not hate. He loves good things for all people and was honest in his conduct. When trusted he does not betray or lie. If he promised you he would not break his promise or deceive you.

\Tailor Ali does not change. He jokes on his way to work or sitting at his sewing machine. He used to exchange funny words with his female neighbor Al-Howad and imitate her husband Wad Umbokol. When he looks at Awlad Hamad Wad Abdulraheem – his cousins – they flee fast fearing his comments and descriptions.

Ali used to have special relation and share secrets with the honorable Sheikh Al-Haj Ahmed Wad Kurdi. They used to speak softly between Al-Khalwa (a religious school for memorizing Holy Koran and learning Arabic language), well, and the row of large water jars.

Ali used to share pleasure and sadness with every one in Al-Kumur. He used to receive returnees to Al-Kumur and farewell leavers. He heartily loved Al-Kumur's gatherings and Souk (market).

Tailors in Souk Al-Kumur have attitudes towards tunes, music, and songs. They love education and modern things. Mohammed Ahmed Umbokol was the first to buy a big lantern where people love to gather around him when he lights it. Al-Amin Al-Mubarak is very active and in constant roaming. Awad Ahmed Al-Najar is his opponent in playing cards. When Awad wins he says to Amin: "stand up. Go and look for a shirt to sew." When Al-Amins wins he says to Awad: "stand up. You wasted your time. By now you could have repaired a table."

Al-Amin was light and used to move briskly. He perfected swimming and dates palms climbing. (Saad ibn Al-Waqqas, "a companion of Prophet Mohammed (PBUH)," used to pollinate and hoe date palms and his brother was a carpenter. The reference is Al-Mahasin and Al-Adhadh "Merits and Opposites" book of Al-Jahiz, page 93.)

Chapter (12)
The Nile is Taking and Offering

Practicing commerce and trades in Souk Al-Kumur is a kind of gaining, hobbies, and self satisfaction. Haj Mohammed used to come from the east, from Salwa Village, followed by his sons Ali and Sulaiman. They used to come on the backs of donkeys. Customers gather around them because of their attraction in commercial transaction and speech.

They used to help the needy and participate in the building of mosques, schools, and hospitals. Haj Mohammed's family has commercial ambitions. Sulaiman left for Al-Buhairat (lakes) and the source of the River Nile for commerce between Central Africa and South of Sudan. But the Nile was fatal at the source and Sulaiman disappeared!!

His brother Ali transferred his commerce to Omdurman. He owned a land plot in Souk (market) Omdurman. He went to East Asia and imported textiles from Indonesia, China,

Taiwan, and Japan; in addition to different types of perfumes from Kirla and Punjab.

Ali Haj Mohammed did not forget his roots. He expanded in buying agricultural lands in Salwa Village, Al-Bawaleed, and Al-Jiraif. He was always talking about the days of Souk Al-Kumur, the days of Mahmoud Wad (son of) Saeed and Awlad (sons of) Atbara Ata Al-Manan and Hussein.

Commerce was established on the equivalence of the Sudanese Pound to the Dollar, Sterling Pound, Yen, and Riyal. Syrian and Jordanian (Al-Sham region) commodities were balanced against Lira and Dinar. Ali Haj Mohammed spent a lot of money on procuring farms in Salwa Village on the side of the same Nile that took his brother Sulaiman.

Mohammed Abdulraheem who was the Leader of Merchants and known as Siqair used to come from west of Souk Al-Kumur. He used to sit down while the buyer takes his commodities and pays him the price. He used to utter some words with each buyer and a joke that stirs laughter among the people who usually gather around him.

Monday's Souk (market) opened its doors for buyers, brokers, and peddlers. Mohammed Wad Abdulraheem Siqair rode his donkey from Hajer Al-Tair heading for the market. The Nile flooded as usual in mid August every year. Water overwhelmed Al-Karo and covered a part of Al-Omdah's (mayor) stones regarded as a berth where some Arabs come down to irrigate their camels and donkeys, and load water on them.

At the berth and near to Al-Omdah's stones one of the Arabs shouted: "hey Wad Abdulraheem! Hey you Siqair! Hey man! Beware of the camel.)

Siqair turned and the camel came running towards him with a red ball dangling out of his mouth and scattered white saliva. The camel was growling and hitting the ground with its hooves. Siqair was quick-witted though he had a heavy body. He jumped off his donkey, waded some steps in the water, and sat on Al-Omdah's lap.

The grumbling and fuming with rage camel stopped near Siqair who was retained by water. After the camel completely calmed down, Siqair raised his head and said to the camel: "come on, proceed on, and do what you think you can do!!"

Thus is the Nile. It took Sulaiman, offered a lot to his brother Ali, protected Mohammed Siqair, and held back the Desert's ship (camel).

Chapter (13)
West of the Souk
House of Al-Hajah bint Zainaldeen

West of the Souk (market) includes the court, Animals Market, Slaughterhouse, and house of Al-Hajah bint Zainaldeen.

Hamad Wad Rahamah and Mohammed Wad Jubarah entered the market from east; and Ali Wad Siddiq from the gate of the slaughterhouse carrying a slain young she-goat.

Mohammed Wad Jubarah calling: "hey Ali Wad Siddiq, how are animals in the market?"

Ali Wad Siddiq: "by Allah, they are butchered from ear to ear."

Hamad Wad Rahamah asking" "are they in the court or slaughterhouse?"

Ahmed Abu Safah stretched his neck suddenly from one of the stores: "hey people, neither the court nor slaughterhouse. They are in the house of bint Zainaldeen."

Bint Zainaldeen secured herself by the court and her business were active in the Animals

Souk (market). Butchers, brokers, and others enter her house. The slaughterhouse used to provide her with legs of animals and bellies. The cottage changed into a big and wide house with a hall. The assembly hall assigned for the native liquor she excelled had also expanded.

All kinds of meat used to be brought to her from the slaughterhouse, butchery, and sometimes animals are slaughtered within her house. Youths of neighboring villages and some visitors of the Souk used to visit her. Merchants and butchers, with all delicacies of meat, used to gather in her house.

Bint Zainaldeen repented in her last days, performed Hajj ritual (Islamic religious obligation for those affording it), and thus called Al-Hajah bint Zainaldeen.

The Court

The court was built west of the Souk (market) with its windows opening at the Animals Souk and house of Al-Hajah bint Zainaldeen. In front of the court there were properties of Sheikh of the Line (of villages) and Omdah (mayor) Youbi - sons of Sheikh Ali Jadallah.

The court consists of three rooms; one for the Omdah of Al-Ja'liyeen, another for Omdah of Al-Shaygiyah, and a third for the clerks, where Saror and Bashir Mahjoob, the clerks of Al-Shaygiyah and Al-Ja'liyeen respectively, are found.

The building of the court is lofty. You can go up through staircase. The front hall is based on pillars with arches on top similar to the ancient Greek style. At the top of the pillar, there is the Oqlah - what the Greeks call 'flower'. The arch is based on the two flowers of the adjacent pillars. The perpendicular cuts the arch into two equal parts and also the distance between the two pillars on the ground.

The brick thick-walls of the court were built on the west landscape of the market. The court made events and history during the native administration by terminating discussions and cases. Disputes were also solved. Conspiracies were woven in the house of Al-Hajah and evidences were proved in the Animals Souk (market). All these affairs were settled in the court or under the mud house of bint (girl of) Zainaldeen.

There were fierce political battles between Al-Shaygiyah and Al-Ja'liyeen during the courts of the native administration at the Turkish and British eras. Titles, ranks, and orders such as Bey and Pasha were distributed from Khidaiwi in Turkey. They used to come from the Sublime Porte in Turkey to Mohammed Ali Pasha, Ruler of Egypt, which was then a Turkish colony too. The Turkish Ruler in turn used to send it to Sudan.

Some members of Al-Shaygiyah tribe obtained titles such as Hashim Bey and Al-

Turky Ahmed Mohammed Khair. The waterwheel inherited by his grandsons was called Al-Turky's waterwheel. His nephew Ali was also titled Ali Pasha. Mahmoud, Idris, and Ahmed - Awald (sons of) Saeed – were his grandsons. The later is called Al-Turky. He was a religious Sheikh and scholar. He built a Khalwah for the memorization of Holy Koran and the Arabic language in Al-Kumur.

The British handed the Sheikdom of Line (of villages) to Al-Ja'liyeen under the chairmanship of Wad Al-Bay (son of Bey) in Al-Matamah. He was called Nazir (superintendent) i.e. the responsible for the Sheikhs of the Line (of villages) and Omodiyat (plural of mayordom). Ali Jadallah, the Sheikh of Line (of villages) of Al-Kumur's district and administrations, was under Busharah, mayor of Al-Shaygiyah.

The Sheikh of Line (of villages) and Omdah (mayor) ruled the district cunningly. They were two prominent figures in the political formation of the district. The political hierarchy was made of the Sheikh of the tribe, Omdah, Sheikh of the Line (of villages), and Nazir (superintendent).

The name of Al-Ja'liyeen is linked to Ali Wad Jadallah, who represents the head of the ruling party in the district. The number of Al-Shaygiyah increased in the region. As a result they desired to dwarf the Sheikhdom of the Line (of villages) or taking it for political and financial reasons related to leadership and distribution of agricultural lands respectively, in the basin of Wad Hamid.

Uprising and revolutionary blocks were formed led by Al-Shaygiyah. They overwhelmed all villages of the region and were a mixture between Al-Shaygiyah and Al-Ja'liyeen. Al-Quraishab, a branch of Al-Shaygiyah, came to Al-Kumur's court, blockaded the court, and prevented officials, subordinates, and police from entering it.

A young man called Abadi, from Al-Shaygiyah, wearing a black cloak and riding a black horse appeared in front of Al-Kumur's court; going around and shouting.

"I am the black, in black, riding a black horse, and looking for the black day."

Shandi police station sent an additional police force to the court to keep order. During these events, Ali Jadallah's family left to Hajar Al-Tair Village. The best candidate to counter the events and lead the family of Ali Jadalla was his son Mubarak, who tried to open the court for the men of the native administration.

These were the events of the mid 60's that preceded the military coups in Khartoum at the end of the 60's, which made the Sudanese people suffer a lot of the struggle between the military and sectarian parties represented by the Omah and Khatmiyah Parties.

Afterwards regional events in Al-Kumur's region and other regions disappeared and followed political movements in Khartoum.

Mubarak Ali Jadalla had to follow the policies of Khartoum parties. And Taj Al-Sir

Bashir, another candidate, appeared. The region was drifted to another wider side deriving its power from Khartoum and where the nominee could find a way to serve his region. As a result election processions, votes, and interests went behind those who would serve the region. Bit by bit the native administration and tribal affiliations disappeared.

In the wake of education, conditions changed and generations fused by marriages. Mubarak's mother and his first wife, who was the half sister of Taj Al-Sir Bashir, also were from Al-Shaygiyah tribe.

Thus politics took its toll among the cousins in the region same as the spree of buying and selling in Souk Al-Kumur which ends with sunset and Maghrib (sunset) prayer collectively behind Khalaf Wad Al-Fadul. It was not a question that Imam could be from any tribe. The most important thing was to perform a complete prayer.

Hamad Wad Rahamah said while standing behind the Imam: "please Sheikh, make the prayer light." When the prayer was over they joke, ask Allah forgiveness, and disperse.

Strangely enough, these tribes invent jokes from politics. Happy occasions bring them together. They sit down to eat from one plate as if they have no differences between them. Serious matters change into jokes even inside the yard of the court.

Balah Wad Al-Fadul filed a case against the court's buildings and that they were built on this family's lands. He got the Sheikh of the Line (of villages) and Omdah into a thorny case that the people regarded it as one of his endless jokes. They ridiculed at him and excused him for going out. He refused and Sheikh of the Line (of villages) called the bailiff: "Al-Duboli, please drive this man out."

The bailiff put his hands on the back of Balah and pushed him out. Balah turned his body backwards, moved his feet briskly, and went out of the court. He danced at the court's door, jumped, raise and shook his hand, and got into the market.

Different kinds of wild and tamed birds flap their wings at sunrise and before sunset. They land, fill the square of the market looking for obtainable subsistence, and pick scattered seeds inside and outside the Souk (market).

The domesticated pigeons spend their day in Souk Al-Kumur. When it was too hot, they enter the verandahs and settle on the muddy store pillars. Some of them live near the market, fly with food to their off springs, and come back many times in the day.

The wild pigeons (Baloom) avert the market when brokers come in, fly to the top of mountains and valleys, and follow sand grouses that used to fly in early morning. They pick their food briskly, drink at Abu Jamal berth, and fly deep into the Desert and Al-Sadah (masters) Mountains.

There are also the cow birds and storks that divide to the east and west of the market. From the west on the edges of Al-Karo, the storks head to Hajar Al-Tair (Mount of Birds) and Wad Al-Habashi (son of the Abssinian). To the east towards Sawarid and Um Bagarah, the cow birds fly.

Hawks and falcons exit from the western gate near the slaughterhouse to Um Zor. And some of them fly to Al-Tarjamiyah heading towards trees loaded with Khuraim and Olaif plants.

The grey-colored small birds land on their nests on top of the mimosa and acacia trees in the valley near the market.

Two birds remain on top of the highest branch of the old Harazah tree; on the dividing line at the intersection of sand and mud below the market towards Al-Karo.

From here starts a divider between mud and sand; a thin thread towards the Nile that inclines in a curve at Al-Samani's shop and Al-Jodaliyah Canal. Then down to Al-Sheait's tree at the tip of Al-Mamlouk land to enter the Nile at the bore of Mohyidden tree. It is the dividing line between the Nile and Desert.

Every atom of sand has a tale, and each seed has a soil. Two adjacent trees; one very green, leafy, and thick branched to the right of the divider. The other – stemmed from the sand - with a dry trunk, light leaves, and two birds on top of it; one old and feeble, and the other was fat.

The Animals Market

Ali Wad Siddiq put down the slaughtered young she-goat. Hamad Wad Rahamah and Mohammed Wad Jubarah stood before him.

Ali Wad Siddiq: "lift with me this animal for Al- Shankal (hook)."

Mohammed Wad Jubarah: "your young she-goat is fat, by Allah."

Hamad: "thank Allah for the safety."

Ali Wad Siddiq: "by Allah, there is absolutely no safe road between west of the market and butchery!"

At the Animals Market donkeys bray, young she-goats bleat, and lambs play. Sheep stand quietly except for sudden sighs and hit their heads with their flapping ears. Bellies of animals round and atrophy, legs tied, and necks extended downwards or on shoulders of others. They are quiet harnessed for circulation, obedience, and slaughter.

The broker comes along, his hands playing with his pockets, and followed by a buyer who examines with a harsh movement the posterior and backbone of the sheep, opens its mouth, examines fatness of the front legs and chest, tail, pats it once or twice, and drives it away. He says: "selling and buying are based on: "May Allah opens the gates of profits, and: "May Allah protects." (Usually the buyer offers a price and if the seller does not agree to it then he says the former part, and the buyer says the latter part.)

He takes the sheep to the slaughterhouse at the back of the court and in front of the house of Bint Zainaldeen. He slaughters it and hangs it with hooks. On the floor of the slaughterhouse blood flows and clots into the sewerages. Animals' heads are put in the cloth or leather bags. Indeed there is absolutely no safe road between west of the market and the butchery!

The goat shuddered itself and entered the Animals Market after taking a mouthful of the heaped stuffs. The owner of the last heap, stroke it with a stick. Merchants decided to go to the court. They agreed to warn the female owner of that goat. That goat was lucky enough not to be dealt with the butchers' knives, glanced with the eyes of brokers, or enter the house of Al-Hajah Bint Zainaldeen.

Zainab bint Hamzah decided to lead her goat to the agricultural lands and waterwheels to graze for some time and return back. As the goat was used to these agricultural lands, bint Hazah left it this time also to go down alone where plants and seeds.

The goat was used to seize opportunities of harvest and collection of seeds in Al-Taqa (place for accumulating crops in the farm), which looked like the scene of the market. It practiced its activities and hobbies by introducing its mouth and front legs into a heap of seeds, eat, disperse them, and run away from one heap to another.

Farmers complained of this naughty goat as merchants did before them. So her female owner kept it away during the days of harvest and Al-Nuraiq (collection) in the next year. When people collected their harvest and the season was over, days of unleashing animals had come. They were allowed to pasture on whatever remained on the ground.

Bint Hamzah released her goat. The goat took off towards the farms with its ears in straight line beside its head, piercing the ground with its hooves of the two front legs together and simultaneously, tucking up its stomach, and curving its back so that its hind legs replaces its front legs in the run. It stood on top of Al-Tarad Mountain.

The goat took a panoramic view to determine the place to attack. It decided to attack the middle land of Al-Turky waterwheel. It quickly got down and started running around in all directions. Alas, there was nothing except the soil and ruins. The people had collected every thing. The goat had missed every thing.

The goat supported its body on its four legs, raised its front legs, and left its body high for some time with the lower cloven hooves opened as if its head was hooked in the slaughterhouse. Sent a long bleat, fell to the ground, and died!!

This Nilotic goat preferred to die beside the Nile. Her female owner was one of those who migrated from Al-Doshab. The goat finally left the market for the gatherings of expatriates.

"Hey brothers, take us with you to Saudi Arabia."

"Saudi Arabia is over and there is nothing in it."

Al-Nur: "you have reaped it all together?"

Al-Sir: "by Allah, if you go to Saudi Arabia, what has occurred to the goat of Bint Hamzah will befall you."

They all leaned on each other, as usual, while laughing and each one is hitting the shoulder of the one next to him.

"Get up guys."

"Where to?"

Al-Sir: "to Manfouhah (an ancient quarter in Riyadh City in Saudi Arabia)!! Where do you think we will go? Let us go to the folks of Umbokol and play whist."

"Tonight Al-Kumur launched its mortar guns."

Then the group dispersed.

After the end of expatriation, some of them returned to the land of the Two Niles and some to Souk Al-Kumur, which some of its walls were ruined. Hasabalrasool got married to a girl from Awlad Al-Saqr, from the Arabs of Al-Tarjamiyah. He disappeared from the Souk. The word of "your account is paid" disappeared too; and the word "sharing" appeared.

The Slaughter house

The slaughterhouse is a scene for the yearning of Africa and wailing of the Arabs.

On its floor, cows bellowed and camels grumbled. The pillars of the slaughterhouse are erected on a hill inclining towards the gorge that separates it from the Animals Market. The hooks of the slaughterhouse are dangling as gallows where hoofs, bones, and what is emptied from the bellies of animals are dispersed underneath.

There are heaps of black stones, on the rocky road that extends from the slaughterhouse to the butchery and into the market known as Al-Mazlagan (slipper). On the yard of the slaughterhouse eagles perch, hawks land, cats mew, and dogs bark. They compete for the remains of slaughtered animals.

Movements of butchers are endless between the Animals Market, Slaughterhouse, and the Grand Market, except when they enter the house of Al-Hajah bint Zainaldeen to quench their thirst.

Here, in the slaughterhouse, camels, cows, and sheep are slaughtered. Billy goats and young she-goats are hanged. Some blood flow and other is dry, wet, or solid.

Abdulqadir and Khalafallah moved from Al-Kumur with cows and calves to Nasri Island narrating the morning stories and crossing the land of the slaughterhouse.

The oxen smelled blood, stopped, yearned, raised their nostrils, inhaled, dropped their heads, sighed, a latent current of sadness went through them, moaned, exchanged high moos, and heavy tears came down of their eyes. The two men were affected. The cows moved around, rubbed their nostrils on the pillars of the slaughterhouse, and got together lamenting the land of Africa.

The oxen bellowed, and cows inspired and shed tears. The sides of their bellies moved out and in till the ribs are clear. The two men looked at each other amazed and absentminded. At that moment it seemed as if the whole creatures in the world wept silently and the universe was overwhelmed in deep sadness.

Abdulqadir felt the sadness of the livestock and wept as well. He chided the cows with abnormal gentleness as he was suffering awful pain and burning in his heart.

Khalafallah pulled the rope of the cows. They stopped moving, complied, and lined up. They moved towards the fine line separating between sand and mud, which inclines away of Al-Sheait's tree, towards the Nile.

Al-Sheait Wad Muntaha died in Um Zor where the Arabs and nomadic groups wept him. His daughter bint Ashmanah went around the coffin, before it was carried on the shoulders, urging him to make the journey of adventure that follows the rainy season and saying poetically: "oh father, stand up *Karab* (echoic word describing the act of standing up suddenly); the people has headed for *Jarab* (a place).

People were packing their things preparing to go and cultivate the rain-irrigated lands in Jarab. Um Zor natives love camels and feel proud of them. If someone dies, women as usual, follow the coffin when it comes out. Camels trot behind them growling.

Mohammed Ahmed Wad Al-Sheait maintained his camels. One day he made his way through the Slaughterhouse Road to his farm with a camel behind him and a leashed she-camel behind that camel. The camels suddenly knelt down on the land of the slaughterhouse pressing their chests against the ground. They made such a growl that indicated a deep sadness; as if they were weeping the camels slaughtered on the hill of the slaughterhouse.

Wad Al-Sheait said: "what a ruin world! Everything is perishing and transient." The camels crept on the floor of the slaughterhouse, pressed their chests against the floor and growled. Tears dropped from their eyes and blood from the back of their heads.

Mohammed Ahmed said: "move up, and let us go." The camels moved their hocks slightly backwards, raised their posteriors, pulled their front legs forwards, and stretched their necks inside the valley. They proceeded through the edge of the sand screen inclining towards the left. To the right there were palm, lemon trees, and creeping grass undulating on the ground.

Farmers were calling each other loudly and making gestures. Some of them cursed and called bad names to a she-goat that went around its stall and said: "may Allah take you to west of the market."

The eternal struggle goes on between land and mountains. Mohammed Ahmed says: "by Allah, we don't know. Are we inheriting the earth or the earth is inheriting us?"

Idris replies: "see how many people cultivated this land, from the Turkish era till now? Nevertheless they passed away and left the land?"

Mohammed Ahmed: "men left this land and passed away, glory to Allah!"

Idris bent to the ground, stretched his hand and started Yukadiq (hacking small grass). Mohammed Ahmed was also Yukadin (hoeing grass) from the canal. Immigrant names mixed with original ones on the land of the Nile.

Mohammed Ahmed's camels approached the Nile to drink. They drank as if they never did. These 'Ships of the Desert' are brought from the valleys to the Nile.

The gathering of camels was coincided with Abdulqadir and Khalafallah leading a herd of cows and calves. Thus immigrant animals coincided with original ones on the land of the Nile.

Wadi Abu Hawiyah sands got down to the Nile at Mohyideen's gorge. They formed the gap of the natural desert. Al-Tarad also came down to Al-Karo as an artificial gap. Migrant nature yearns to the Nile water.

Three families own the land between the natural and artificial gaps. These families are: Awald (sons of) Mohyideen, Awlad Al-Mulook (kings), and sons of Al-Turky. The land of the Nile brought together Mohyideen, the immigrant Arab, and Al-Turky, the non-Arab immigrant, and Mulook Al-Nil (Kings of the Nile). It also brought together the migrant human beings, nature, and animals.

Chapter (14)

The Daily life Drama between the Cataracts

The procession of nature, human beings, and animals advanced towards Souk Al-Kumur. The Nile flooded highly with its blessings embracing trees and touching the sand at the market. The people, old, youth, and children came out of Al-Kumur. Birds perched and all animals moved: cats beside rats; rabbits and dogs beside lambs. And under the trees tortoises and reptiles crawled. So human beings applauded.

Flocks of birds flapped their wings above the Nile water. One of them separated itself from the flock, turned its head, focused its eyes, brought together its wings, dived skillfully into the Nile, snatched a fish, and flew back into the air.

A kite perched on the courtyard. The colored pieces of cloth stretched on a rope did not prevent it from snatching a young chick. Children followed it with their sad eyes. The sound of the chick gradually faded away and the chick got smaller and smaller. The dust was stirred, ropes were shaken, and clothes fluttered and calmed down.

The kite turned to the east. Spread its wings and perched somewhere between the valley and mountain on an old tree. The kite chose one of the dry branches and landed on it. The bird fidgeted and with a quick move changed places of its claws on the body of the young chick. The chick calmed down and two light plants dropped from its neck. The kite hit twice with its beak and went on changing its claws from one place to another. Snatched once or twice of the chick's body and stretched its curly neck. It turned around, tightened its claws on the remnants of feathers and blood, pressed downwards, and the branch yielded. It flew up and the branch resiled on the Desert thorny tree piercing the air.

One grown up child said: "hey men, first we will build a den for the chicken, stretch ropes to prevent invaders, and cut the tail of those who make the chicken stay awake all night.

Second, we will not snatch the Nile's fish to die in the air or leave our birds to be killed above the Desert's trees."

From under the old sheet iron, at the kitchen corner, the hen came out crowing. Its incubation period was over and the young chicks followed it. It led them into the valley as rolling cotton balls.

Their legs were shaking. They tumbled and got up. The mother crowed and they responded. When it scratched the soil with its claws, they gathered around. It picked the ground with its beak and they attacked looking for food. They used to go around it and scramble, climb on its back, tilt and fall, and raise their feet from the heat of the sun.

Their yellow wings were short, bored bills were red, and little smooth and transparent bellies dangled. They live between the Nile and Desert.

The old man cleared his throat after hours of sweltering heat and calmness at midday, and washed his face. Life started to creep gradually into the body of the village. Soon rays of light would radiate slightly between the branches of Awlad Wad Ahmed's forest and the shadow would cast eastwards.

The children would shout in the shadows, playing Al-Aytnoba, Haraina, and Ala Al-Mes Jaraina (to the finishing line we ran).

It was four o'clock, the old men started to gather in the shadows of shops and Khalawis (religious Islamic schools). Farmers were preparing seeds for cultivation. Al-Dagoy (the young nursing rabbit) started to play, infants dally, young men seduce, and Al-Muntalab (young nursing calves) struggle. It was the twilight.

The sun went down. People of all ages and games gathered beside the Nile. They got into the Nile to swim. One generation floated and the other dived. They got into the Nile naked, but the Nile clothed them. They swam, and what a sport is better than swimming? And what a friend is better than the Nile and the bank as a companion?

Conclusion

The Nile River is divided into three sections in the Nuba land: water, desert, and mountains. The Nilotic animals follow these divisions. The Nuba land is also divided according to the wild animals.

When the Nile recedes in summer, islands appear with their sands as a Nile desert. The cataract's stones become a river mountain. Water runs between them and go around the annual islands.

Nilotic animals follow the Nile divisions. Tortoises live in water and desert islands. They crawl slowly on the hard rocks, as they are elements of diversity of place. Fish swim and a she-crocodile lay two eggs on the island.

On the course of the Nile, between the mountain rocks and islands, water runs eastwards. But there is another river of the Desert sand, which runs in the opposite direction, westwards and then southwards, advancing on the edges of the White Nile to become two seas (rivers) in Southern Sudan:

Bahr Al-Arab (Arab Sea) and Bahr Al-Gazal (Gazelle Sea), so that Arabism and Africanism become the culture of Sudan.

It remains to say that the Nile is a river, but in the Arabs' culture it is a sea; as they are amazed of the abundant fresh water as they are knowledgeable of seas and not rivers.

"Oh sheikh, this is a sea, this is a sea!!" "No, it is a Nile, man!!"

Glossary

Abu Hawiyah: name of a sand valley in Al-Kumur floods with rain storms.

Al-Karo: the dry muddy soil

Al-Kakar: a wooden stool on which Nilotic tribal kings of Fung and people of Sinar in central Sudan used to sit on it.

Al-Hafir: artificial low land to store rain water

Al-Maharaib: aromatic desert herb.

Al-Mohar (oysters): Nilotic shells with small living creatures.

Al-Kokaraj: an evil creature in games and tales.

Al-Hugah: small snuff tin box.

Al-Mardal: means disease and the last 'L' are for a curse of "may Allah inflict you with it."

Ykadiq: to hack small grass.\

Yikadin: to hoe grass from the creek.

Yetailan: irrigate his plants for the second time.

Al-Aroti: part of the waterwheel where water pour.

Al-Ashamiq: a rope interweaved from the bark of palm trees.

Al-Tuga: a place in the farm for accumulating crops

Al-Tagawi: seeds.

Al-Dagowi: a young nursing rabbit.

Al-Muntalab: a young nursing calf.

It remains to say that the Nile is a river, but in the Arabs' culture it is a sea; as they are amazed of the abundant fresh water as they are knowledgeable of seas and not rivers.

"Oh sheikh, this is a sea, this is a sea!!" "No, it is a Nile, man!!!"